To Our Seven Children:
(The Family Blend)

Wedding Day, August 18, 2017

Within the pages of this book, we share more than words—it's a collective journey through life's unpredictable terrain. A path where the echoes of loss have mixed with the richness of laughter, the depth of love, and the enduring threads of legacy. Along this road, we've encountered unexpected detours, each turn reshaping our path in ways we hadn't planned for. Your bravery in navigating this landscape of change is nothing short of inspiring.

To you, we dedicate 'The Grief to Growth Pathway.' This is more than a dedication—it is a heartfelt thank you. Thank you for the dimension you've added to our lives, the lessons you've taught us, and the extraordinary privilege of being your (bonus) parents.

We Love You

Chapter 1

Introduction

As we prepared to stand on the stage of a church in South Florida, Kari and I exchanged a nervous glance. While we often spoke to audiences and shared stories about the challenges and quirks of blending our large family — two girls from my side, five boys from hers, drawing chuckles and inevitable "Brady Bunch" comparisons — this event was unique.

My college friend Gordon was the pastor of this church and had invited us to share with his community. He wanted us to talk about our distinct journeys of loss: Kari's sudden loss of Eddie and my agonizing walk through the throes of cancer and losing Marybeth. As the weekend approached, a whirlpool of emotions from our past engulfed us. Ordinary conversations turned tense. Sleep evaded us, replaced by vivid dreams. Disagreements sprouted from the most unexpected corners. Why now? Was this the grief that we thought we had processed resurfacing?

A common misconception is that once you've moved into a new chapter in life, like remarrying, the symptoms of grief should vanish. Yet, as we've learned, grief isn't a linear path you simply leave behind. It affects every facet of existence: physical, emotional, cognitive, and spiritual.

After sharing our stories that weekend, a swarm of emotions greeted us as attendees approached. One lady, tears streaming, recounted the loss of her son. "What is your son's name, and do you have a picture of him?" I asked. As she beamed and showed me the photograph, I realized that sometimes people need permission to say their loved one's name and cherish their memories. They don't need advice or profound wisdom, just a listening ear and the reassurance that their loss and emotions are valid.

A man, new to the congregation and still mourning the loss of his wife, approached us next. During our talk, we emphasized we weren't trying to "move on" FROM our grief but were instead "moving forward" WITH it. He confessed his guilt, feeling like he was on the cusp of a new chapter in his life. Our words had provided him with a comforting vocabulary, a way to honor his late wife while acknowledging his developing journey.

The stories from people in the audience that weekend continued. Some shared the heartbreak of miscarriage and disrupted adoption, while others dealt with career shifts and unrealized dreams. Loss, as we discovered, wears many faces. One of the greatest misconceptions is that grief only results from the death of

a close loved one. People have told us, "I can't be grieving...no one I know has died recently."

As our plane cut through the skies back to California, we reflected on these stories, feeling deeply moved. Our journey had transformed from simply navigating our grief to helping others find their path and pursuing growth and healing.

A Compassionate Guide

The Grief to Growth Pathway emerged from our heartfelt commitment to guide those who've felt the weight of losing someone or something significant in their life. We understand that the journey of grief is as unique as a fingerprint. Each path is distinct and shaped by individual experiences and emotions. As we've walked through our various losses, we hope you read this book in your own journey, filtering each page through the lens of your personal experiences.

While we aren't here to dictate a 'right' way to grieve, we want to shed light on the nuances of the process. We do not intend to prescribe a path, but to make the terrain more recognizable. Our experiences have taught us it's possible to take the next step forward with purpose, not by forsaking our grief, but by weaving those poignant memories and lessons into our life's story.

As you explore the following chapters, remember: even as we share our stories, the narrative is truly about you. Consider this

book a gentle companion, offering insights and perspectives as you chart your course from grief to growth. Your story deserves to be honored, recognized and used as a beacon for future steps.

Chapter 2

The Stormy Seas of Grief

A Fateful Day in Gulf Shores

T he excitement was tangible as our family prepared for what was to be a beautiful destination wedding in Gulf Shores, Alabama. My nephew's wedding had given us the perfect opportunity to gather. Our families had traveled from different parts of the country and stayed in two neighboring beach homes, creating a mini-reunion.

From the deck of our home, you could see the stunning white sands of the Gulf Shores. The crisp air and calm waters were the perfect setting for the beautiful wedding ceremony. The following day would be filled with a flurry of activity as we made final preparations. However, we received weather alerts of an incoming

storm. Optimism led us to believe it would all blow over, but the skies had scripted a different narrative. The storm escalated with each passing hour, morphing into urgent hurricane warnings and whispers of evacuation that sent ripples of concern through our families.

Faced with the weather's unpredictability, we knew the ceremony wouldn't wait another day. With a resilience that perhaps only a close-knit family could muster, everyone rallied. The change wasn't just accepted; We embraced it with cooperation. Amidst the whirlwind of rearrangements, the wedding took on a new shape, marked not by disaster but by the beauty of adversity. On the morning after the wedding, we witnessed the display of our collective strength. We awoke to furious winds, and the gulf's waters became a turbulent sea of churning waves. Trees bent in distress, and the air buzzed with the fury of the incoming hurricane.

This turbulence wasn't just a meteorological event; it was a moving parallel for life's unpredictable storms of grief and loss. Reflecting on this event, I am reminded of how quickly circumstances shift. One moment, life is a portrait of perfection, and in the blink of an eye, calm is overshadowed by confusion. It emphasizes that peace isn't the absence of turmoil but the ability to find it within the storm. Experiencing grief can be highly disorienting. Like a hurricane's unpredictability, sadness and pain can surprise us. To move through these emotions demands resilience, bravery, and self-compassion.

Understanding Grief: Natural Yet Intricate

Grief is the heart's raw reaction to loss. It embodies the intense sorrow and void felt when something or someone cherished is no more. Imagine grief as an uninvited guest: sudden in its arrival, unwelcome in its persistence, and capable of turning your life upside down.

While everyone encounters grief, its impact varies from person to person. There is no "right" or "wrong" way to grieve. Your individuality, cultural background, personal history, and the bond you shared with the departed molds your journey. For some, grief's emotions hit immediately, while numbness or disbelief may consume others at first. Acknowledging the uniqueness of your loss is crucial for healing.

Grief can produce a chaos of feelings. Beyond sadness and despair, it's common to grapple with anger, guilt, anxiety, loneliness, fatigue, bewilderment, and even numbness. These emotions can oscillate rapidly or linger longer than expected. However, understanding these feelings as typical—even in intensity—can ease potential guilt or surprise.

Grief isn't solely an emotional battle; it affects the body, too. Changes in appetite, disrupted sleep, diminished energy, and even physical pain can surface. Pre-existing health issues might intensify. During this challenging period, prioritizing your health through rest, balanced nutrition, and physical activity is fundamental.

Tune into your body and mind's needs, treating them with care. Remember, your feelings are valid regardless of when or how they surface.

As we delve deeper into the turbulent waters of grief, you might find yourself caught in its powerful undercurrent. Yet, we want to reassure you: there is hope. Whether navigating your loss or supporting someone close to you, the upcoming sections will introduce the significance of frameworks in our lives. These frameworks can offer guidance and hints for your subsequent steps. We urge you to maintain an open heart and mind as you move forward.

Harnessing the Power of Frameworks

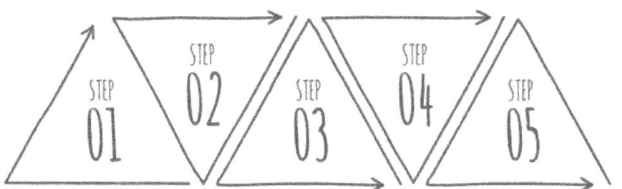

The Role of Frameworks in Our Life

In its broadest sense, a framework refers to a basic structure or set of steps someone can use to achieve an aim. Frameworks give order to chaos. They help break down complex processes

into manageable steps, allowing us to move forward, even when faced with uncertainties. Think of a framework as a scaffolding—providing structure, guidance, and support as we rebuild. We often rely on frameworks to plan our day, organize our thoughts, or set goals. They are essential tools for making sense of things and providing clear paths toward resolution.

Embracing a Grief Framework

One of the most challenging aspects of grief is its unpredictability. While the grief journey is personal, understanding its impact can help you better expect, understand, and manage your emotions. Just as we would consult a weather report before embarking on a sea journey, familiarizing ourselves with the grief framework can provide insights into the challenges we might encounter. While grief is deeply personal, having a framework can serve as a guide. Knowing the stages or patterns of grief won't eliminate the pain. Still, it can help prepare and equip you with strategies to handle emotions more effectively.

A grief framework does not prescribe a one-size-fits-all solution, nor is it about rigid boundaries or a "set of rules." Instead, the framework offers a structure and sequence to better understand and process grief. The goal is to provide some predictability amidst the storm, helping you see that there is a horizon—an endpoint or at least a smoother journey ahead. Let's look at some widely accepted frameworks for grief and loss.

Five Stages of Grief: A Closer Look

Dr. Elisabeth Kübler-Ross, in her influential book, On Death and Dying, pioneered our understanding of grief. In 1969, she presented the world with the five stages of grief: denial, anger, bargaining, depression, and acceptance. These stages, while not in a strict sequence, provide grieving individuals with a roadmap during their most challenging times. Since then, many have adopted this definition as the standard for the grief process, so let's examine it more closely.

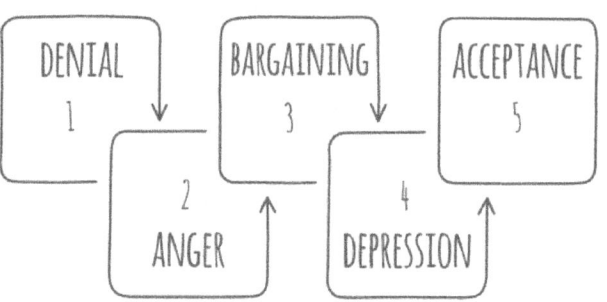

Stage 1 Denial

This initial stage serves as a protective shield, cushioning the immediate shock of the loss. Imagine it as your mind's way of saying, "This can't be happening." It gives you a brief respite, allowing you to process the harsh reality at your own pace. In this

stage, you might find yourself immersed in distractions or even feeling a disconnection from the world around you. Understand that this is a natural coping mechanism that will develop with time.

Stage 2 Anger

As the protective layer of denial fades, anger often surges. It's an emotional expression of the intense pain you're experiencing. You might ask, "Why me?" or direct blame toward others, medical professionals, God, or even the significant person who died. This anger can co-exist with feelings of longing or deep sadness. Embrace this emotion, understanding that it's essential to the healing process.

Stage 3 Bargaining

The desire for control manifests in the bargaining stage. Thoughts like, "What could I have done differently?" or "If only I had been there," might dominate your mind. It's a desperate attempt to find answers or make sense of the loss. But remember, it's all too easy to fall into the trap of guilt and rumination. Instead, acknowledge these thoughts, understand their origin, and gently steer yourself towards self-compassion.

Stage 4 Depression

Here, the weight of grief becomes genuinely tangible. It's the realization that there is a finality to your loss. Symptoms like frequent crying, a desire to isolate, sleep disturbances, and a disinterest in daily activities can be overwhelming. It's essential to understand that this isn't a sign of weakness but a natural phase of grief. It's the heart's way of acknowledging the deep nature of the loss.

Stage 5 Acceptance

Reaching this stage doesn't imply you're "over" your loss. Instead, it symbolizes recognizing your new reality and the first steps toward healing. You might find moments of peace and joy as you slowly rebuild and find purpose. Embrace this newfound perspective, understanding that it's a developing process that will bring hope and resilience.

Kübler-Ross's Five Stages of Grief has helped countless grieving individuals validate their experiences and find footing in chaos. Best used as a loose framework, not a rigid map, your grief is unique. There is no perfect sequence or timeline. Give yourself permission to feel and experience it fully. With its multifaceted and deeply personal nature, grief doesn't fit neatly into boxes or stages. Kübler-Ross's model paved the way, offering solace to those grappling with overwhelming emotions, suggesting they

were not alone in their journey. However, grief's complexities extend beyond five stages, as subsequent research and personal experience have shown.

Since then, many models and perspectives have emerged to capture the depth of the grieving process. Each offers a distinct lens through which we can view grief, and together, they enrich our understanding of this powerful human experience.

The Four Tasks of Mourning

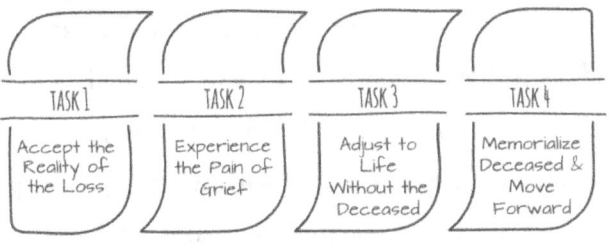

Mourning often gets portrayed as an ebb and flow of emotions. However, another lens through which you can view this journey is as a sequence of tasks. Rather than merely waiting for the pain to subside, you actively engage in specific actions that help facilitate your healing process. J. William Worden's "The Four Tasks of Mourning" presents such a framework, suggesting deliberate steps to help rebuild your world after experiencing loss.

Task 1: Accept the Reality of the Loss

The first task involves acknowledging the magnitude of your loss. Accepting that your loved one is no longer present might seem unthinkable, especially when the pain is fresh. Yet, to heal, you must grasp the finality of this reality. You step closer to acceptance when you talk about your loss, share your feelings, or even sit quietly with your memories.

Task 2: Experience the Pain of Grief

Diving deep into your grief's emotional landscape is therapeutic and essential. Embrace every emotion, from sorrow and anger to guilt and confusion. Suppressing these feelings stalls your healing journey. Instead, express them. Whether you write them down, share them with someone, or turn them into art, make sure you let them out. It's through this expression that emotional processing and healing take place.

Task 3: Adjust to Life Without the Deceased

Losing someone often means adjusting to a life where roles change, routines shift, and new skills need mastering. Perhaps your loved one used to handle certain tasks or filled specific roles in your life. Now it's time for you to learn how to live in this reshaped world. Writing a list of these changes and individually addressing them offers clarity and empowers you to take control.

Task 4: Find Ways to Memorialize the Deceased and Move Forward

Holding onto memories and honoring your loved one doesn't mean getting stuck in the past. Celebrate their life by visiting special places, creating memorial spaces, or adopting new rituals. While cherishing these memories, you also pave the way for the next chapter in your life, ensuring your loved one's legacy continues alongside your personal growth.

Worden's Four Tasks of Mourning framework is not just about navigating the aftermath of death but applies to various types of losses. Whether it's the end of a relationship, losing a job, or even a significant change in life circumstances, these tasks offer a proactive approach that brings a sense of purpose and direction.

Navigating Grief and the Power of Connection

Grief Literacy: Understanding Your Emotional Voyage

Life inevitably brings us face-to-face with loss, and the ensuing tide of grief can easily engulf us. But here's a beacon of hope: grief literacy. It's not just a term. Grief literacy is about wrapping our minds around the countless emotions that loss brings, swinging back and forth between them, and directing them positively. When thrown into a storm of sadness, anger, and confusion, it's crucial

to steer through those emotions instead of trying to shut them out. Grief literacy whispers a gentle reminder: you're not alone on this turbulent sea. Others have navigated similar experiences, and your emotions are a real, valid part of the journey.

This is Personal

Every person's grief journey is deeply personal and unique. Your grief might stem from significant losses, like the death of someone close or the end of an important relationship. But remember, even what might seem like smaller transitions—like moving houses, switching jobs, or adapting to a new environment—can also unleash powerful feelings of loss. There's no "right way" to grieve. Every path you tread is significant and valid and deserves recognition. Sometimes, we might forget to acknowledge the grief that comes with transitions not related to death. But the emotional upheaval from moving away from loved ones or adapting to a new culture is just as valid. Giving room to these emotions is crucial.

The Lighthouse of Support

Your support network, like a steadfast lighthouse, guides you through your grief journey. Connecting with friends, counselors, or family who provide genuine feedback and a safe space for your emotions can be life-changing. However, it's also vital to remember that relying solely on others isn't the solution. Making

self-care a priority—whether through exercise, mindfulness, or introspection—builds your strength on this journey.

Balancing Digital and Personal Connections

In our modern world, the digital realm offers various pathways to express and navigate through your grief. I am thankful for how social media has allowed Kari and me to remain connected with friends and family who live in different parts of the world. We have also received timely encouragement and support when it was much needed. The danger lies in substituting these online interactions with in-person connections. Social media, while enabling us to connect with others, share experiences, and receive condolences, can also trigger grief emotions. For some, the reminder of significant dates or broken relationships can be difficult to manage. We must balance the benefits with the understanding that social media can lack the deep emotional connection required during times of grief.

The warmth of physical presence and real-time conversation is unparalleled. It provides depth and authenticity that might not be possible through digital connections. Not that online support is not beneficial, but the power lies in finding balance in our relationships. In times of loss, this is pivotal.

The Undertow

Living in Orlando, Florida, introduced me to the cautionary world of "red flag" days. These warnings, frequently broadcasted on the news, signaled danger at the beach. We'd sometimes go to Cocoa Beach on our leisure days, soaking up the sun and enjoying the fresh air. However, the sight of those red flags altered our plans, showing a rip current.

Rip currents are a peculiar yet dangerous phenomenon. They possess the deceptive ability to drag you further into the ocean, often without you even realizing it. One moment, you're near the shore, and the next, the coastline is just a distant view, with the relentless tug of the current preventing a return. Local news often emphasized that the safest way to escape the forceful grip of a rip current isn't to head straight back to shore—even though that feels like the most logical action. Instead, the recommended strategy is to swim parallel to the shore, a direction that might initially seem counterintuitive.

Loss and grief behave much like these rip currents. They can pull us into an ocean of depression, making us feel lost and disconnected from the world we once knew. Navigating through this turbulent emotional sea requires an approach that might appear indirect or unexpected. As with the rip current, confronting grief head-on isn't always the best approach.

Sometimes, we must step back, analyze our surroundings, and find a fresh path toward healing and growth.

The Journey Continues

Throughout this journey, it's crucial to remember that grief's overpowering tide recedes with time. The surge of sorrow weakens with patience, perseverance, and the occasional willingness to swim in unexpected directions. New horizons emerge, offering opportunities, renewed hopes, and fresh dreams. Each step, no matter how small or seemingly out of direction, is a part of the healing process. As we walk this pathway, let's remind ourselves of the importance of patience, resilience, and the belief that brighter days await.

While uncomfortable, there's strength in vulnerability. Seeking support isn't a sign of weakness; it's a testament to your resilience and commitment to growth. Embracing self-compassion is not just a buzzword, but a genuine practice that nurtures your soul. Whether that means journaling, seeking therapy, joining a support group, or simply talking to a loved one, ensure you're taking steps to heal. In chapter five, we will examine what self-compassion means and how to integrate it into our daily lives.

Know that you stand at a significant crossroads. Upon reflection, a collection of experiences, emotions, and memories unfolds. As we set our focus ahead, there lies a winding path full of potential for discovery, understanding, and growth. As we approach the

following chapters of this book, we will explore the "Grief to Growth Pathway," guiding you through its six phases. This transition serves as a reminder: Even in the extreme depths of grief, there lies an opportunity to rise, transform, and thrive.

Copyright © 2023 by Matt and Kari Perkins

All rights reserved. No portion of this book may be reproduced in any form without written permission from the publisher or author, except as permitted by U.S. copyright law.

Grief to Growth® is a registered trademark. Unauthorized use of this trademark is prohibited.

The author of this book does not dispense medical advice or prescribe the use of any technique as a form of treatment for physical, emotional, or medical problems without the advice of a physician, either directly or indirectly. The intent of the author is only to offer information of a general nature to help you in your quest for emotional, physical, and spiritual well-being. In the event you use any of the information in this book for yourself, the author and the publisher assume no responsibility for your actions.

Paperback ISBN: 979-8-9895998-0-6
Ebook ISBN: 979-8-9895998-1-3

I0532327

The
Grief
to
Growth
Pathway

A Guide for Transforming Your
Loss into Renewed Purpose

MATT AND KARI PERKINS

Contents

Chapter 3

The Journey

From Grief to Growth

Discovering The Grief to Growth Pathway

In the vast landscape of grief, one can feel an overwhelming sadness with no apparent way out. As we journeyed through the previous chapter, we laid the foundation for understanding the multifaceted nature of grief. We explored various frameworks and delved into some established models. Kari and I will guide you through the Grief to Growth Pathway, a method born from our individual yet parallel stories of loss.

The Synchronicity of Our Stories

Life has an uncanny way of bringing souls together through shared pain. When Kari and I first met, we had endured the indescribable pain of losing our spouses. But what surprised us was how our tales of love, commitment, and loss eerily mirrored each other. We met our late spouses during our tender teenage years, made lifelong commitments at 19, and dedicated our lives to ministry work. It was more than just shared grief; it was the shared journey of our lives, the emotions, memories, and love that transcended our individual stories.

The weight of our grief, intense and profound, extended beyond ourselves. It resonated with our children and the congregations we were part of. They, too, mourned alongside us, feeling the void left behind by our departed partners.

As time went on, our paths merged further. We found love and understanding in each other, leading us to the sacred bond of marriage. With the blessing of our combined seven children and the support of our late spouses' families, we embarked on the next chapter of our lives. It is important to note that our grief didn't stop just because we remarried. With each step forward, we recognized the importance of addressing grief for ourselves and the countless others facing loss. The echoing questions from others became impossible to ignore. "Is what I am feeling normal?"

Crafting The Pathway

From this deep realization emerged the Grief to Growth Pathway. We felt an immense responsibility, not just to guide people on "how to grieve" but to offer a sanctuary of understanding.

We aspired to craft a guide with more than just steps to follow. Our dream was to create a comprehensive approach that addresses the spiritual, relational, vocational, and restorative aspects, illuminating the interconnectedness of loss.

We urge you to embark with an open heart as we navigate the Grief to Growth Pathway phases. Kari and I want you to hold on to one truth tightly: your story isn't over. Sometimes, the world seems to close in, and despair feels all-consuming. Believe me; I've been in those depths. Yet, remember, traveling this pathway requires courage and introspection. While challenging, it's a journey infused with hope, possibility, and a strong potential for growth. With every sunrise, your story develops, taking fresh turns and revealing unforeseen horizons. Embrace the journey, for your story is still being written today.

The Pathway

The juncture at which Kari and I pondered our future, the idea of marriage, and the potential challenges it might involve was overwhelming. For someone like me, who tried to foresee and navigate the complexities of life, leaping the unpredictable was intimidating. It felt as though I was venturing into an unknown territory with no understanding of its design.

A Lesson from Scavenger Hunts

In times of uncertainty, a particular memory from my high school days took on deep significance. I remembered the excitement of our church youth group's scavenger hunts. We would eagerly start from the church, with nothing but a clue guiding us to our next destination. The thrill wasn't just in the discovery but in the journey. We discovered early on that skipping clues or taking shortcuts would leave us lost, having missed a crucial part of the journey. You would have to retrace your steps to where you deviated to find your way again.

The parallels between those scavenger hunts and our personal grief journeys were uncanny. Just like the hunt, the urge to hasten the process or skip stages is apparent in grief. However, doing so only prolongs the anguish. It's essential to tackle each phase head-on, no matter how daunting.

Introducing the Grief to Growth Pathway

This realization birthed the Grief to Growth Pathway—a beacon in the unexplainable storm of grief. This approach illuminates the journey from anguish to understanding, loss to purposeful progression. Allow this book to guide you, like a compass, toward your next essential step.

Our collective experiences and insights from therapists, psychologists, and countless others who've walked this challenging path resulted in a six-phase process. This roadmap clarifies the volatile terrain of loss, assisting you in recognizing your grief, processing emotions healthily, and, ultimately, guiding you toward hope, healing, and personal growth.

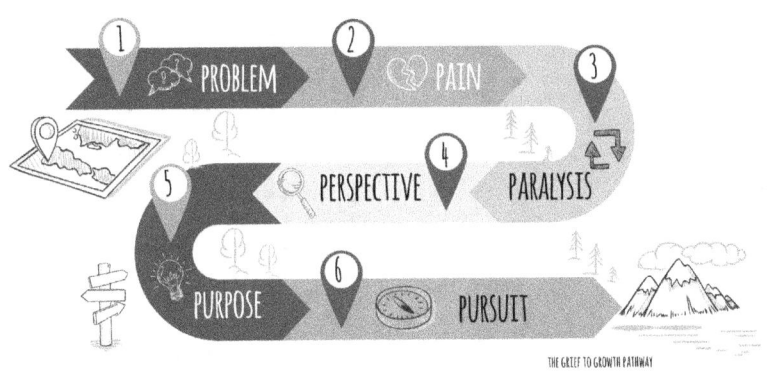

THE GRIEF TO GROWTH PATHWAY

Six Distinct Phases

We use the term "phase" to describe the six Grief to Growth Pathway markers. We can define a phase as "a distinct period in the process of change or development," providing a semblance of structure and order to the inherently chaotic nature of grief.

The six distinct phases of the pathway are:

1. **Problem:** Recognizing the root of your grief.
2. **Pain:** Acknowledging and feeling the emotional impact.
3. **Paralysis:** Understanding the moments of stagnation.
4. **Perspective:** Gaining a new viewpoint on the journey.
5. **Purpose:** Discovering the meaning behind the journey.
6. **Pursuit:** Moving forward with newfound wisdom.

By breaking down the process into six phases, we offer a roadmap that does not oversimplify the journey but acknowledges its intricacies and provides a language to articulate its progression. This not only aids in understanding and validating one's feelings, but also offers guidance in navigating the winding path from sorrow to meaningful growth.

Phase 1: Problem

From the moment we are born to the day we take our last breath, we will face various forms of loss. And every loss brings with it its unique set of emotions, reactions, and challenges. The first phase in the Grief to Growth Pathway I have appropriately named the "Problem."

These moments bring us face to face with a loss, whether it's the heart-wrenching death of a loved one, the painful end of a marriage, the unexpected loss of a job, or any other life-altering event. Shock and denial become our immediate companions. The world seems to shift under our feet, the sky a shade grayer, and making sense of the chaos feels impossible. Everything seems surreal, like watching a movie in one's life rather than living it. This disorientation is not just expected; it's natural. It's the mind's way of coping, protecting, and navigating through unexpected waves.

During this time, it's essential to give yourself permission to feel, emote, and wade through the myriad of feelings without judgment. Pushing emotions away or bottling them can lead to prolonged pain and potential complications in later phases. We often try to make sense of experiences by relating them to what we know or have seen. In doing so, we make assumptions about grief and how it manifests.

Two prevalent assumptions when grieving:

1. Everyone grieves like us.

2. No one grieves like us.

Ironically, these contradictory beliefs can exist simultaneously in our minds, but both are myths. Grief isn't a one-size-fits-all journey. Every individual grieves in a manner unique to their personality, experiences, and the nature of the loss. Recognizing this is essential. It reminds us to avoid the trap of comparisons and to approach our grief and the grief of others with understanding, empathy, and patience.

As we move through the Grief to Growth Pathway, understanding the nuances of each phase, starting with the Problem, equips us to navigate our journey with resilience, hope, and a belief in a brighter tomorrow.

Phase 2: Pain

As we maneuver the Grief to Growth Pathway, the second phase, aptly named "Pain," is perhaps one of the most extensive and challenging phases. This is the juncture where the numbing haze of shock clears, and the stark reality of loss becomes palpable. The gravity of what we have lost seeps in, often accompanied by a whirlwind of powerful emotions ranging from extreme sadness and anger to guilt.

With its raw, unfiltered intensity, we can sometimes liken grief to fear, as so eloquently described by C.S. Lewis in *A Grief Observed*: "No one ever told me that grief felt so like fear." [1]

The nature of grief is not linear nor uniform; it ebbs and flows, and the experience is as unique as our fingerprints. The vast sea of emotions you navigate during this phase is entirely natural. They are an inherent part of our human design, developed as

---

1. Lewis, C.S. A Grief Observed. Faber and Faber, 1961

mechanisms to process the harrowing trauma of loss. These emotions serve dual roles. They are our tools for coping with the immediate aftermath of loss and the avenues through which our hearts and souls mend.

Marc Brackett, in his book *Permission to Feel: Unlocking the Power of Emotions to Help Our Kids, Ourselves, and Our Society Thrive*, wisely observed: "If we don't express our emotions, they pile up like a debt that will eventually come due."[2] This statement underscores the critical importance of acknowledging and expressing our feelings. Much like a pressure cooker, they build up if we leave our emotions unchecked. They can eventually erupt, often at the most unexpected or inopportune moments.

It brings to mind the adage, "You can pay now or later, but either way, pay." This wisdom holds especially true when addressing the myriad of emotions accompanying loss. We must remember emotions are NOT the enemy. Instead, they are signals, communicators of our internal state, striving to bring our attention to something that needs addressing. Emotions can rise to the surface without warning and become overwhelming. But by recognizing, honoring, and expressing them, we open pathways to understanding, acceptance, and healing.

---

2. Brackett, Marc. Permission to Feel: Unlocking the Power of Emotions to Help Our Kids, Ourselves, and Our Society Thrive. Celadon Books, 2019

As you navigate this phase, be gentle with yourself. The pain you feel is directly proportional to the meaning, joy, and comfort your loss brought you. With such deep love comes the potential for deep pain when it's withdrawn. Be brave enough to look into that pain's eyes, cry out in anger, or curl up in sadness. These expressions aren't signs of weakness but evidence of the meaningful connection you're grieving. Through acknowledging and exploring that bond, you gradually incorporate this loss into the rhythm of your everyday life. Even though it will etch itself into your heart, your loss will gradually transform into a mix of bitter and sweet memories.

Phase 3: Paralysis

Like an animal caught in a trap, struck by an immobilizing fear, you may come to a halt in the grief process after weeks or months of painstaking forward movement. This third phase of the Grief to Growth® progression is when feelings of being emotionally trapped or stuck predominate. You may sense a complete inability to adapt to your new reality post-loss. Where once you made steady progress through the grieving process, now doubt, anxiety, and depression consume you each day.

Why does this paralyzing overwhelm descend just when healing seems within reach? The initial shock has worn off, allowing you to comprehend the true magnitude of this life-altering change. The stark reality of a future without someone or something cherished becomes painfully clear. You desperately long to return to what was, yet know the way back is not possible.

Caught between an unbearable past and an unfathomable future, you freeze—unable to function or envision a life without what you've lost. Weeks or months may pass in a haze of barely surviving or simply going through the motions. You understand the reality of your loss, but can't fathom how to move forward. You may become tangled in depression, anxiety, prolonged anger, or numbing routines that distract from core emotions that demand expression.

Recognize that this paralysis serves a purpose. According to renowned psychiatrist Elisabeth Kübler-Ross, "Depression after a loss is too often seen as unnatural or a failure to 'get over it.'[3] The first thing to know is that grief and mourning rarely progress in an orderly, stepwise fashion. And depression in response to a loss is normal." This period of extreme challenge provides an opportunity to fully accept how altered your old reality and identity have become. By delving into that darkness, you can locate the inner resources to assemble a new reality and identity that integrates your loss.

This phase demands courage and patience—with the process and with yourself. Confronting and paralyzing emotions and envisioning a new life are challenging work. Don't underestimate

---

3. Kübler-Ross, E. (1969). *On Death and Dying*. Macmillan.

the enormity of what you're being asked to do. Each minor act of engagement with your feelings, each tiny stride forward, plants seeds of hope.

Phase 4: Perspective

When deeply entrenched in the despair and stagnation of grief, even the mere thought of moving beyond it feels like a far-fetched dream. A pivotal moment arises for many who dare to embark on the intricate journey of introspection. This moment heralds the onset of the 'Perspective' phase in the Grief to Growth® process.

In this phase, we acknowledge the unwavering reality of the loss. The protective shields of shock and denial have receded. While the loss remains unaltered, its inner resonance transforms. It's understood that while time might not be the magical balm that heals all, it is the lens that offers perspective. This enlightenment doesn't dawn overnight. It germinates from acknowledging and expressing one's emotions related to the loss, understanding the unique nature of the experience, and embracing the complexity of life's difficulties.

As one navigates through this phase, loss grows from a mere focal point of anguish to an instigator of enriched perspective, burgeoning wisdom, and individual growth. We recognize loss as a significant chapter in the sprawling epic of one's life, no longer the overpowering narrative it once was in the initial throes of grief.

This transformative juncture integrates grief into your present and envisioned future. The loss becomes a thread in the intricate weave of your identity. We honor its memory through anniversaries, traditions, artistic expression, or contemplative rituals. However, the gaze has broadened, accommodating the entirety of your essence and the renewed purpose ahead.

As the days unfold, one discerns the perplexing dance of grief. It pushes you into the embrace of joy, pain, love, and isolation. It echoes the sentiment of poet Rainer Maria Rilke...

> *"These are not two friends that walk together; these are two friendly enemies that, by walking and talking in a certain friendly way altogether, avoid a standstill."*
>
> Rainer Maria Rilke

In its relentless manner, grief beckons us to keep journeying, engaging in dialogues with these eternal companions throughout our life's maze-like path.

Phase 5: Purpose

Grief, often perceived as a destructive force, has a transformative side. The introspection and personal growth it fosters can lead one to understand life's value, fragility, and the potential for renewed purpose. After braving the stormy seas of loss and emerging from the cocoon of healing in the previous phases, the "Purpose" phase is where the mosaic of meaning appears.

As you've passed through the painful landscape of loss and sorrow, you perceive life through a redefined lens. The gravity of your loss prompts more sincere questions about life's essence: Who am I now? What is my renewed sense of purpose since being changed by loss? How can I craft a life that embodies the lessons and love experienced throughout this journey? How do I plan, based on the depth of my wisdom and understanding from this loss, to craft a life that embodies the lessons and love I experienced throughout this journey, ensuring I always cherish the love and memories shared? You acknowledge the indelible mark left by your loss, yet there's empowerment in deciding how it influences your path.

In this phase, your heart and soul might guide you toward new horizons. Some draw to activism, philanthropy, or community service, their loss and insights driving them. Others find renewed zeal in their existing professions or relationships, seeing them as a testament to the strength and resilience they gained from the impact of loss. Crafting tangible memorials like traditions, rituals, or monuments anchors shared memories and love, offering catharsis.

Many discover a sense of purpose in externalizing their transformative journey. Be it through writing, painting, music, or any other form of art, these expressions are personal testaments to resilience, serving as lighthouses for those navigating grief's turbulent waters. By transforming individual pain into a beacon of hope and guidance for others, you lighten your spirit and contribute to the collective healing for those in your community.

Phase 6: Pursuit

Arriving at the Pursuit phase signifies a monumental shift in the Grief to Growth Pathway. This is where you stand tall, invigorated with the wisdom carved from the trenches of sorrow and loss. Once a dark presence, grief now emerges as a transformative ally in this phase. As with many relationships, the raw and overwhelming emotions felt in the initial stages of grief strengthen into milder and more sincere reflections. As time passes, grief transforms into moments of contemplative sadness and presents opportunities for growth, providing compassion, resilience, and purpose.

Your relationship with grief, currently, isn't about moving on or leaving it behind, but moving forward with it as a cherished part of your being. You make choices and decisions through the lens of the wisdom that grief has given. Whether chasing after dreams, immersing yourself in passions, or championing causes, everything resonates with the new clarity and depth of understanding the delicate mix of joy, pain, and love. This integration of loss into your identity creates a beautiful balance where joy and sorrow coexist. Moments of joy emerge, easing the weight of guilt and offering comfort in acknowledging loss while moving forward.

The rhythm of grief remains, even as we actively and passionately engage with life. It is essential to understand that its presence is fluid, moving in waves. Rituals and customs become meaningful anchors, reminding you of the significance of your loss. As life marches on, birthdays, anniversaries, or even random memories can cause an unexpected surge of emotion. But these aren't setbacks; they're gentle taps on the shoulder, affirming the eternal bond of love. Grief's wisdom, permanently inked in your soul, provides the strength to welcome these emotional surges, letting the richness of memories offer comfort.

As the pages of time turn, grief's jagged contours become more mellow and worn. Your heart's vast expanse accommodates a beautiful blend of hope, possibilities, and cherished memories. This insight into the human experience, painted with the colors of loss, makes you navigate life's journey with unparalleled patience, presence, and purpose. The essence of the Pursuit phase is the powerful realization: While the loss may have reshaped you, it has, in no way, diminished your spirit.

Applying the Grief to Growth Process to Life's Challenges

The Grief to Growth Pathway provides an invaluable framework for navigating loss. While commonly discussed concerning grief, this process can adapt to all painful life transitions. Any change involving the irreversible loss of someone or something significant demands grieving. Applying this framework to other losses allows you to honor the grief experience fully and ultimately emerge renewed.

This model offers orientation through tumultuous times, whether it's the end of a relationship, losing a job, the onset of a chronic health condition, infertility, or a dramatic change in ability. The phases give structure to diffuse emotions and guidance for constructing new meaning amidst radical life changes. While each loss bears unique hallmarks, the overarching process for traveling from heartbreak to healing remains similar across experiences.

Relationships Ending

Few losses rival the intensity of a severed intimate relationship. Whether it's divorce or a breakup in dating, the end of a once-cherished partnership leaves you reeling. Your sense of identity and day-to-day life undergo a fundamental disruption. You may cycle through phases of the Grief to Growth Pathway over months or years following the relationship's end. But by understanding critical guideposts in this terrain, you can mindfully process the chaos of change.

Shock and denial predominate initially, as the full implications of this loss register. The person who once offered comfort is now the source of wounding, leaving you raw and disoriented. Navigating legal processes and custody or untangling shared property multiplies the stress. Prioritize emotional wellness while avoiding any major decisions during this unstable period.

As denial lifts, painful emotions flood your psyche. Anger, regret, abandonment, and heartbreak may crash over you unrelentingly. The life you knew feels decimated. Be extremely patient with yourself during this agonizing phase. Find healthy outlets for expressing this intensity through physical activity, counseling, or communication with compassionate friends.

The paralysis phase makes you numbly struggle to imagine your solo future after the relationship. Loneliness and depression might immobilize you. Engage your support system by taking small, daily actions to affirm your progress. In time, perspective emerges, allowing you to see the relationship's end as only one element of your broader story. Appreciating this loss as part of your more extensive growth process is brave, soulful work. Ritualizing this passage through writing, artwork, or ceremony can be powerful. Share your hard-earned wisdom with others undergoing similar struggles.

As purpose forms, the desire to live authentically in alignment with your values surfaces. Make choices honoring who you've become through this pain. Pursue education, service, or community engagement, expressing your renewed spirit. Ultimately, let the brokenness you have experienced become a catalyst toward embracing life's fullness with an open heart.

Job Loss or Change

Losing a job can shake your sense of financial stability and identity. The sudden loss leaves you untethered, whether it's downsizing, company closure, termination, or quitting because of toxic conditions. Applying the Grief to Growth framework helps restore equilibrium.

When shock sets in, it dulls the nerves that would otherwise respond with fear. Job search mode ignites your survival instincts, propelling you forward. As you attempt to grasp the enormity of this change, a sense of dismay lingers beneath the surface. Strengthen your resilience by adopting healthy habits and minimizing extra stress during this challenging period.

The sheer pain of losing your livelihood soon follows. Anger, humiliation, anxiety, and sadness may crash over you. The job often held deeper personal meaning connected to vocation, community, and self-worth. Take time to fully grieve these intangible losses through honest conversations with loved ones, career counseling, or therapeutic support.

Paralysis paralyzes progress when the job search drags on without results. Self-judgment, hopelessness, and stagnation stall momentum. Combat this through scheduling regular activities, exploring alternative career directions, or considering entrepreneurial options. Small steps forward renew the energy and optimism needed.

As time goes by, a shift in perspective can illuminate the possibilities born from this loss. Or maybe you realize just how many transferable skills you possess. This vision propels your purpose.

You redirect wisdom gleaned from the loss into tangible goals. Returning to school, launching new businesses, or pursuing that creative passion stoked by the loss becomes entirely possible. Suddenly, you feel called to help mentor others transitioning after a job loss, volunteering with career networking organizations. From the ashes of this unexpected life change, a purpose can emerge.

Health Shifts

Experiencing a shift in health can be incredibly difficult, both emotionally and physically. A newly diagnosed health condition or disability can bring about feelings of grief and anger. Whether it's a cancer diagnosis, organ failure, injury, or debilitating illness, losing health recalibrates nearly all aspects of life. The Grief to Growth process offers an anchoring framework amidst fear and uncertainty about the future.

Initially, there may be some sense of shock that provides insulation from the harsh reality. However, as denial fades, emotions like anger, sorrow, and resistance surface prominently. It is important to practice patience and take care of yourself while seeking support to process these complex emotions.

Acknowledging and mourning the loss of your physical abilities is an incredibly painful but necessary part of this journey. Seeking counseling or taking part in group discussions where you can express your fears, disappointment, and concerns is both courageous and constructive. Showing compassion towards yourself will empower you throughout this trial. During the phase of paralysis, where everything may seem impossible or lost, it is crucial to address feelings of depression, isolation, and disengagement from life with care. Taking steps forward each day can help restore hope and momentum. Remember that this condition is one aspect of your entire being and purpose.

Over time, perspective may emerge, which allows you to recognize possibilities within your limitations. Your creativity and resourcefulness will come into play as you build a lifestyle that aligns with your values. The support from your community will also play a role in this process.

You may find yourself inspired to share your experiences with others who have recently received a diagnosis. Or you may become involved with medical research, legislation, or patient advocacy related to your condition. By taking action, you can communicate that certain situations do not define who you are as a person.

Your Roadmap for Life's Inevitable Losses

The Grief to Growth process empowers you to befriend adversity. You learn that loss, though painful, contains hidden wholeness.

It can uncover undiscovered strengths, connections, and callings that propel you forward if you remain open. With courage and compassion, you'll find the light of growth awaiting you, even on the darkest of journeys. We'll all come to know the lexicon of loss intimately throughout a lifetime. Grief remains one of the few universal human experiences. Yet, for all its familiarity, grief's arrival can upend us in the most fundamental ways. We lose not only people or things central to our lives but also parts of ourselves—former versions of identity, hopes for the future, and feelings of stability and control.

The Grief to Growth Pathway offers a roadmap for navigating life's inevitable losses. Understanding this six-phase model gives you essential guidance and validation for the myriad of emotions and challenges grief brings. You discover that heartbreak, while deeply painful, contains a breathtaking potential for awakening and renewal. Step by step, episode by episode, you journey from barely surviving devastation toward embracing survival's precious gifts.

Walking this narrow ridge demands extraordinary courage and resilience. Loss clarifies the brevity and gift of life. No matter where you are in your grief process, have hope that your present anguish will eventually give way to the delicate beginnings of a new chapter.

Chapter 4

Problem

When Faced with Loss

Loss, often labeled "the equal opportunity offender," affects everyone differently. Kari suddenly lost her husband, Eddie, after he spoke on a Sunday morning at their church. This tragic loss touched Kari and their five children and shook an entire congregation that had revered Eddie as their cherished children's pastor for nearly 15 years. In my experience, Marybeth received her cancer diagnosis as my family, and I adjusted to a cross-country move. This shift uprooted our family rhythm, introducing a barrage of doctor appointments and infusions and depending on unfamiliar faces in a new community for support. Merely seven months post-diagnosis, we mourned the loss of Marybeth. Again, in his work *A Grief Observed*, C.S. Lewis articulates the disconnection that accompanies loss, stating, "There is a sort of invisible blanket between the world and me... It is so uninteresting."[1]

So, why name this phase the "Problem"? Isn't the anguish from a loved one's sudden departure, a relationship's end, or the dissipation of a once-vibrant identity self-evidently problematic? We use this term because any transformational journey begins with a challenge or "problem" that ignites a need for change, growth, or evolution. In the Grief to Growth Pathway, the "Problem" isn't merely the loss; it encompasses the emotional and physical aftershocks.

Your loss journey is personal to you. Perhaps you find yourself as a caregiver for a loved one whose health or mental faculties are deteriorating, leaving you guilty of thinking, "This is not the person I once knew." As we journey together on the Grief to Growth Pathway, I urge you to interpret it through the unique lens of your losses—the loss of a job, a relationship, or an identity shaped by life's various transitions. While each loss is uniquely painful and personal, they all echo the universal nature of loss: it's inevitable, painful, and yet transformative.

During this phase, survival mode kicks in, making you feel lost in unfamiliar territory without guidance. The familiar becomes foreign. Yet, this phase isn't solely about turmoil; it's also a time of personal reflection. After a significant loss, thought-provoking

---

1. Lewis, C.S. A Grief Observed. Faber and Faber, 1961

questions confront us about life's purpose, the reason behind our suffering, and more. While answers might elude us, these questions push us to introspect on our beliefs, values, and priorities.

In the "Problem" phase, an overwhelming wave of love, support, and solidarity often manifests. Friends, family, coworkers, and even strangers might extend their support. This painful phase can unveil humanity's innate kindness and empathy. As we journey together, we realize that everyone's path is unique. While some might see their story in Kari's or mine, countless others possess their narrative, each as valid and impactful. Your story and experience might differ from the ones shared here. But as we walk the Grief to Growth Pathway together, recognize that every narrative, especially yours, holds significance. Each story can inspire, comfort, and guide - propelling us towards healing and transformation.

Understanding Types of Grief

Grief comes in many forms, each with unique features and challenges. By understanding different manifestations of grief, you can better identify what you or your loved one's may experience, find resources, and walk the path of loss with greater insight. While these are not the only types of grief, they can give a vocabulary and help you identify with what you may be experiencing. Throughout this book, you will see grief referred to in various metaphors or analogies. The visual image of a storm is often used to depict grief, with its chaotic and unpredictable nature. To better describe the various types of grief, we will also reference a unique storm to give you a mental picture of the impact that it has.

Anticipatory Grief

Living in Central Florida for many years, I became accustomed to the powerful thunderstorms that would roll through every afternoon. One minute it could be perfectly sunny, and without warning, a tremendous storm would blow through. I was riding my motorcycle home from work on one of these afternoons. Because there weren't any clouds in the sky, I left my rain gear in the storage compartment. Getting closer to home, I saw the warning signs ahead. Like it or not, I was going to feel the impact of this storm. Much like the gentle mist that served as my warning, anticipatory grief envelops us silently, hinting at the extreme emotional upheaval awaiting us. This form of grief emerges not from a loss that has already occurred, but from the looming shadow of an impending one. It could manifest as someone witnesses the slow decline of an aging spouse, watches a loved one grapple with a terminal illness, or even in significant life transitions that herald an end to familiar patterns and relationships.

This preemptive sorrow isn't just a preliminary stage to the more 'conventional' grief that follows a loss; it is its own complex journey of the heart and mind. While it offers time, allowing for moments of reflection and meaningful goodbyes, it doesn't guarantee relief from the depth of grief that follows.

Complicated Grief

In the first chapter, I shared the story of a hurricane approaching while we were in Gulf Shores, Alabama. In the context of complicated grief, it roars into lives, becoming a tempest that doesn't merely pass but permanently alters the landscape of one's emotional world. This metaphorical hurricane doesn't allow individuals to endure it as a passing storm. Unlike conventional grief that might gradually dissolve, this formidable, emotional tempest, also known as prolonged grief disorder, staunchly resists the passage of time. It becomes a powerful force, where every attempt to progress feels like battling against forceful winds, pushing them deeper into a desolation that overshadows every aspect of daily life.

This is more than feeling sad for a period. Complicated grief manifests in ways such as despair and being consumed by thoughts of the departed loved one. There may also be bitterness towards the circumstances of the loss. Some people struggle to accept that the loss actually occurred or believe that life has no purpose without their loved ones. They might avoid memories or places, experiencing loneliness, or engaging in risky behaviors as they seek comfort or escape their pain.

If the grip of complicated grief lasts six months or more, seeking help is crucial. By seeking support, individuals caught in the complexities of their situation can start untangling it, gain a perspective, and rekindle a sense of purpose on their journey.

Disenfranchised Grief

Envision the feeling of isolation as you stand amidst a brutal winter storm, the gusts of wind making it hard to stay upright. The landscape is barren and offers no shelter or relief from the chilling winds. This imagery expresses the solitude and pain of disenfranchised grief. Like a winter storm, this type of grief isolates and constricts, rendering their sorrow unnoticed and unacknowledged. This chilling desolation mirrors the deep loneliness experienced in disenfranchised grief. This pain remains hidden and often invalidated by society. It's a grief that arises from losses that, for various reasons, don't receive public acknowledgment or societal support. Such grief can result from various losses, each as deeply felt as the next. There's the silent despair of undergoing a miscarriage, the tangled sorrow that arises after the passing of an ex-spouse or a distant relative. Some experience the muted anguish of losing a beloved pet, while others grapple with the emotional turmoil from job loss or the extensive identity shift that follows personal illness or disability.

Amidst such grief, many find themselves isolated, struggling to express their pain or find validation. This enforced silence often means emotions become suppressed, making closure seem out of reach. For true healing to begin, these individuals need a sanctuary — a place or community that observes, acknowledges, and validates their pain. Only with such understanding and recognition can the heavy burden of disenfranchised grief dissipate, paving the way for genuine mourning and recovery.

Cumulative Grief

Picture yourself standing on the shore, feeling the strength of one powerful wave crash against you, and then being bombarded by relentless water surges one after another. Each wave threatens to knock you off your feet, pushing you further into the depths of sorrow. This unyielding tide is the essence of cumulative grief, where loss upon loss mounts in rapid succession, threatening to drown the spirit in its intensity.

Whether it's the heart-wrenching experience of losing multiple friends or family in a brief window, the shadows cast by severe family illnesses, or the collective grief arising from natural disasters, acts of terror, or economic instability, these successive losses can drain emotional resilience. The combined weight of such grief often complicates mourning any single event, submerging individuals in an ocean of sorrow. Yet, like any tidal force, the key to navigating cumulative grief is acknowledging each wave, seeking ample support, and gradually regaining one's footing. It's essential to take the time to process each distinct loss, allowing for the gradual integration of these experiences into one's life narrative. Through this meaning-making process, one can transform the overwhelming pain of cumulative grief into a purpose, reshaping one's journey and finding strength amidst the surges.

Traumatic Grief

Picture a tranquil meadow suddenly swept up in a ferocious storm, its once serene beauty replaced with chaos and destruction. This sudden, jarring transformation mirrors the essence of traumatic grief, an intense sorrow birthed in the crucible of unexpected and often harrowing losses. Whether it's the abrupt aftermath of accidents, the destructive force of natural disasters, the haunting shadows of heinous crimes, or the echoing horrors of war, these events leave souls grappling with deep and disorienting grief.

Those enduring traumatic grief don't just mourn the tangible loss; they also confront a barrage of intense reactions. The initial disbelief can coat the heart in a sheath of numbness, creating a detachment from reality. Disturbing images and memories may invade their thoughts, leading to avoiding anything that might trigger reminders. Sleep, that gentle healer, can become elusive or overwhelming, and emotional responses might range from heightened anxiety and irritability to depression and guilt.

When grief emerges from such catastrophic events, care providers must recognize the distinct symptoms of trauma intertwined with the sorrow. Tailored interventions, grounded in trauma and grief therapy, can guide individuals on their path to healing. Through these therapeutic journeys, survivors can weave their losses into a narrative that, while acknowledging the pain, also charts a course toward recovery and resilience.

Delayed Grief

Kari and I recently watched a documentary about a volcanic eruption in New Zealand. This island used to attract thousands of tourists each year for hiking and sightseeing prior to the tragic event. I found it interesting that prior to that event, it appeared calm and unassuming, yet harboring a tremendous amount of energy beneath the surface. Like a volcano on the verge of eruption, a storm of long-delayed grief can abruptly overtake a seemingly peaceful heart. Its postponement characterizes this type of mourning, emerging long after the inciting loss. Initially, one might try to suppress the overwhelming waves of grief for various reasons. It might be a survival instinct, a need to push forward in the face of other pressing responsibilities, or even a subconscious desire to shield oneself from the rawness of immediate pain. But, much like a shadow trailing behind us, the grief, though delayed, remains present.

When delayed grief finally emerges, its expression can match the varied and intense nature of grief experienced immediately after a loss. The emotions might seem disproportionate to current events, or seemingly unrelated experiences can trigger them. In its own timing, the heart beckons the mind to process the loss, mourn, and heal. Recognizing and addressing delayed grief is vital. As with any grieving process, creating a space for these deferred emotions is essential, allowing them to be felt, understood, and integrated into one's life journey. With understanding, patience, and support, the once-dormant volcano can find its peace, transitioning from eruption to serene acceptance.

While each form of grief is painful, the ones disenfranchised by society or complicated by additional stressors require extra attention and care. Understanding the various contours gives us language to identify and normalize our individual or our loved one's experiences. There is no singular roadmap through grief, each experience is unique. But identifying your particular grief landscape will help you find the right tools.

Recognizing the Emotions of Grief

When we experience loss, a whirlwind of emotion swirls inside, trying to make sense of our shattered reality. By identifying and understanding these common emotional responses, we equip ourselves with the knowledge and readiness to face the path ahead. While there are additional emotions that we can face, we will take a deeper look at some of the more common emotions that we experience.

Shock and Disbelief

The mind balks in the immediate aftermath of loss, refusing to accept this new and devastating reality. Shock acts as a buffer, gradually allowing the person to absorb the entire pain and integrate the loss. Disbelief similarly shields us against the harsh facts of loss until we can marshal adequate internal resources. Those supporting the bereaved can provide gentle confirmation of the loss while allowing them time and space for reality to sink in. Be prepared for ongoing swells of disbelief and heartache, even long after the loss. The mind protects itself from the magnitude of pain by allowing it only in small doses.

Sadness

When a flood of sadness arrives, it can feel like sinking into a dark pit. Sorrow and tearfulness arise during grieving as longing for the lost person or situation sets in. Crying provides a much-needed emotional release. You may cycle rapidly between sad spells and distraction from the pain. Avoidance slows healing; lean into the sorrow, knowing countless fellow travelers walk this tough road with you. Sadness recognizes the significance of the loss. Allow it to flow, validating the love and meaning attached to what you have lost.

Anger

Like thunder crashing against the hurting heart, anger often erupts during grief. It may infuriate you at the injustice and meaninglessness of the loss. Bitterness may arise towards oneself, the deceased, medical professionals, or even God. Anger alerts us to what needs changing and makes us want to fight for what truly matters. Yet holding onto it prolongs the pain. Release it through safe outlets like physical exercise, writing, and candid conversations. Although you can't undo loss, letting anger fuel you can drive positive changes in your life or community. Channel it wisely.

Fear and Anxiety

The landscape of life feels dangerously uncertain after loss. Anxiety spikes as you ponder an unknown future without someone or something that brings comfort and stability. Fear of losing others close to you may also surface. Anxiety promotes avoidance; resist hiding away or refusing to feel. Check excessive worrying against reality to maintain perspective. During irrational fear, allow yourself to be soothed by supportive loved ones until confidence returns. Anxiety releases its grip as hope retakes root.

Guilt

"If only I had..." Guilt wraps heavy chains around the hurting heart as you replay the "if only's" in your mind. Though guilt signifies you care deeply, misplaced guilt distorts reality. To break free from its weight, list the objective reasons the loss was out of your control. Forgive yourself for the imperfections and misunderstandings that arose. While you cannot change the past, you can still spread the love you wished you expressed while there is time. Detach from guilt by attaching to actions now showing how much you cared.

Relief

That we would experience relief when impacted by loss can appear contradictory and puzzling. But when suffering ends, the lifting of sadness might accompany the loss. Cherish the positive memories and accept uncertainty. Let pain deepen your empathy and find meaning in it. Ultimately, relief gently guides you to embrace life again, encouraging you to embrace new experiences and opportunities despite the emptiness caused by loss. This relief does not erase the grief, but rather coexists with it, providing a temporary respite and guiding the way toward personal growth and healing.

Navigating Physical Reactions

Grief not only stirs our emotions but also triggers various physical responses. As we understand these responses, it can help us confront and manage them with intention. As we do this, it can ease the potential fear and anxiety during these difficult times. Engaging with these physical responses requires a gentle approach that incorporates acknowledgment, understanding, and care.

Sleep Disturbances

While grief drains your energy, many people still struggle to sleep. Anxiety, fear, repetitive thoughts, and physical symptoms like heart palpitations can interrupt sleep. But remember, rest strengthens your resilience in emotional hardships. Combat anxiety by establishing calming routines, reducing caffeine, and considering natural supplements. Engaging in daytime activities encourages better sleep. Give yourself grace, knowing that time can ease these disturbances.

Appetite Changes

Grief can push you to two extremes: overeating or neglecting meals. Opt for small, frequent meals or protein-rich smoothies if you're not feeling hungry. When the urge to binge on comfort foods strikes, choose healthier options. Gradually reintroduce balanced meals, observing how certain foods affect your mood. Mindful eating, even amidst grief, can lift your spirits.

Low Energy and Fatigue

Grief's weight is tangible, sapping your physical energy. Adjust your expectations when energy levels dip. Blend rest and activity to prevent becoming too sedentary. Rediscover vitality by enjoying gentle exercises, nature, hydrating regularly, and gradually returning to beloved hobbies. Navigate periods of low energy in grief with patience.

Headaches, Stomachaches, and Muscle Tension

Grief manifests physically through headaches, digestive issues, and aches in the body. Recognize these as signs to address your health and well-being. Tension builds because of emotional stress, so warm baths and stretching can help ease it. Prioritize relaxation and reduce overwhelming stimuli. Your body demands extra attention in these moments. Familiarizing yourself with these common physical reactions means you can address them without panic. Adopt habits that promote wellness and consult with a healthcare professional if symptoms continue. Your attentive and patient approach will help you during this challenging phase.

Social Withdrawal and Isolation

Grief might convince you that you will never find joy or meaningful connections again, but isolating yourself only intensifies the pain and loneliness from your loss. Resist the pull of isolation by regularly engaging with others through brief chats or strolls with friends. Relive memories with those familiar with your loved one. Join grief support groups to diminish feelings of isolation. Though solitude might feel more manageable, connecting with others can speed up the healing process. Actively guard against isolation. Regularly connect with loved ones, especially during periods of intense grief. Be candid about your challenges and emotions. Let others offer solace and support, even when the pain seems impossible.

Loss as a Personal Journey

Remember that no one grieves the same, even over identical losses. Each carries a unique history, personality, and resources that shape their journey. Some move through stormy pain quickly, while others linger in melancholy. There is no "normal" timeline or prescribed stages, regardless of expectations. Appreciate your emotional patterns, tolerances, and needs. Comparison and judgment only generate more suffering.

How do you best experience release? Angry tears? Quiet reflection? Physical activity? Your wisdom about what heals you runs deep. Listen within. Be patient when progress feels uncertain. Much is happening beyond surface awareness. Each day offers an opportunity to better know yourself and life's mysteries. This journey reveals your stronger, wiser heart.

Integrating Loss into Your Story

Grief forever reshapes your story. However, with intentional care, you can allow your loss to deepen meaning instead of diminishing it. Heal by incorporating your pain into the essence of a life you can cherish. Recall every chapter of your story and recognize everyone who shares it with you. Treasure the memories that remain after a loss. Let your pain open your heart, fostering increased compassion. When you feel your identity cracking, decide how to mold the remaining fragments into a form still brimming with love, joy, and purpose. As we have described the impact of loss, we have used imagery of a storm and the unmistakable debris that can be left in the aftermath. However, with time and care, you can pick up the pieces and move forward. In a life lived to its fullest, even your brokenness, growth can appear.

These challenges will inevitably reshape your viewpoint, values, and vision. Yet, instead of weakening your spirit, you'll see a transformation emerge. Believe in your innate resilience and potential for renewal. You remain the same at your core even amid change—now even more reflective, kind-hearted, and insightful. Embrace these traits, as they amplify the best in humanity. Let your grief illuminate the path for others navigating through their personal darkness. Remember, while everyone experiences grief in their own way, there's a shared wisdom from those who've traveled this path before you. Let their stories nourish you with strength and optimism as you traverse the rugged storm of loss. When life's deepest pains challenge you, remember that you possess all the tools to persevere. If ever in doubt, lean on others for encouragement and strength.

Seeking Meaning and Purpose

In the throes of loss, you might feel compelled to question the very essence of meaning. You may wonder, "How can a kind God permit such pain?" The thought that any good can emerge from your loss may seem unimaginable. If you're feeling this way, I want to reassure you—it's perfectly normal. I still vividly recall a moment during my wife's funeral dinner when someone approached me, trying to offer consolation. They said they had prayed to understand why Marybeth had to pass and believed they had found the answer. It wasn't even a week since her death, and this person felt they had the answers for me. While my first reaction was annoyance, I realized my wife had deeply touched this individual's life, and they were grappling with their understanding of her passing.

Recognize that uncovering the meaning and purpose behind your loss requires time. It might not unfold as you expect. Your healing journey starts when you ask, "What comes next?" As moments pass, ponder on the insights you've gained and the inner strengths you've cultivated. Let your loss heighten your spiritual perception. Cherish those once-overlooked memories of joy before the sting of loss bared your soul. Relive the warmth of their embrace, their infectious laughter. Choose to let love, not despair, define their legacy. To truly honor them, embrace each day with gratitude and mindfulness.

Discovering fragments of meaning can bridge the chasm created by loss. Reflect on what this loss teaches about cherishing the present. How has it enriched your empathy or clarified what truly counts? Let this loss enlarge, not constrict, your heart. Pursue new avenues to serve in their memory. By aiding others in their healing, we transform our pain. Don't seek logic where it might not exist. Some losses aren't clear right away, but as days become years, you discover alternative paths and strengths shaped by your experience with grief.

Grief isn't a chapter that neatly concludes. It fluctuates, constantly shaping you. Over time, gaps emerge between the intense surges of sadness. Gradually, life beckons you back into its embrace. Laughter, once rare, becomes a familiar friend. The loss remains irrevocable, but your spirit—scarred yet enriched by the voyage—persists. You might bear its mark with a limp, but you continue with confidence. Beyond this pain lies the potential for a renewed sense of wholeness.

Chapter 5

Pain

When Reality Sets In

P eople often describe losing someone you love as one of the most painful experiences in life. It can feel like it has turned your entire world upside down, leaving you shocked, heartbroken, and forever changed. After experiencing such a loss, the impact of this life-altering event can weigh heavily on every aspect of your life. It can be incredibly overwhelming to navigate through grief while still fulfilling everyday responsibilities.

Here is Kari's account of when the reality of loss set in.
You know, everyone says the house feels emptier after you lose someone. But you never really get it until it happens to you. It felt like the entire world had stopped by to give their condolences. But then evening came, and one by one, they left. It's when I shut that door

behind the last friend who wasn't staying overnight... It really hit me hard.

I went to each room and told the boys goodnight, like always. Seeing the hurt and pain in their eyes was crushing. There was nothing that could take away their pain. I felt so helpless. I went to our bedroom and just wanted to dive under the covers and forget the day. But as I was tossing the pillows off the bed, it just broke me. He wasn't there... I couldn't even lie on my side of the bed. I slid onto his side. It felt weirdly comforting, but waking up the next morning? That was a whole new level of heartbreak. It was like waking up to the worst kind of reality.

As you face the reality of loss, you may cycle rapidly between numbness, intense sorrow, anger, and disbelief. Triggers that bring anguish and pain may suddenly interrupt moments that seem normal. The deep sadness accompanying loss can have a mental toll on you, making even simple tasks impossible. You may experience symptoms like fatigue, headaches, changes in appetite, difficulty sleeping at night, or even feeling pain in your heart or stomach. The powerful emotions associated with grief can also significantly impact your ability to concentrate, find motivation for tasks, and function effectively at work and in your personal life.

The social consequences of losing someone significant can extend far beyond what meets the eye. It's common for your relationships with family and friends to be strained. You might withdraw socially or get angry due to distress. Even if caring people around you want to support you, feelings of isolation and loneliness can still creep in. It's hard for anyone else to truly understand the depth of your pain or the unique dynamics of your loss. You might even feel you have lost a part of who you are along with your loved one, leaving you unsure of your identity and where you belong.

The impact of loss can bring overwhelming challenges. Regardless of the loss you may have experienced, handling paperwork, legal matters, and financial changes can be incredibly draining. Everyday responsibilities continue piling up, making it challenging to focus and process your loss. Remember to be patient with yourself as you navigate through each moment, hour, and day. The intensity of emotions associated with grief usually reduces in the months following loss. However, it's normal for swells of grief to resurface over the years during milestones, holidays, or triggers. Although the intense pain may lessen over time, you will gain wisdom and understanding as you fully embrace and navigate this process of loss.

Emotional Expression

Many people have grown up in households or cultures that discouraged or even frowned upon showing emotions. I remember the expression that says, "quit your crying or I'm gonna give you something to cry about." While that phrase is commonly used in a joking manner, many people were raised using that as their motto. In order to convey our resilience and competence, we attempt to conceal any emotional response. While we feel we are exhibiting strength, ultimately, we can do significant harm to our mental and emotional health. In addition, when we stuff or repress our feelings, we isolate ourselves from others. Even when we silence our emotions, we must recognize that they do not vanish. They wait. And when they finally get our attention, they often do so with a force that affects us and the people we love most.

The Beach Ball Effect

When we speak on the topic of emotions, Kari offers a compelling analogy that illustrates the perils of suppressing emotions: the image of a beach ball in a pool. Imagine, for a moment, holding a beach ball underwater. The more you push it down, the more resistance you feel. And despite your best efforts, the moment you let go or lose grip even slightly, the ball shoots up, often splashing water chaotically in all directions.

Here's how this analogy mirrors our emotional life:

Pushing the Beach Ball Under the Water: This action represents our consistent attempts to push down, hide, or even deny our emotions. Just as holding the ball underwater requires effort, suppressing our emotions demands a lot of mental and emotional energy. Over time, this can be exhausting.

The Forceful Resurgence of the Ball: When we finally lose our grip on the ball, or it becomes too taxing to hold it down any longer, the ball surges up with a powerful force. This is like the moments in our lives when our emotions burst uncontrollably after prolonged suppression. I remember taking our daughters to SeaWorld when they were young. In some of the shows, there is a clearly marked section of seating labeled as the "Splash Zone." Such outbursts, after suppressing our emotions, can be surprising, intense, and sometimes even overwhelming for us and the people surrounding us. At the moment, we feel that holding back our emotions will show others our strength and resilience. We don't consider that those close to us can be impacted by the "splash zone."

By recognizing the dangers of keeping our emotions "underwater," we can understand the importance of acknowledging, processing, and healthily expressing our feelings. Emotions can be channels for growth, understanding, and deeper connections with others when dealt with openly and honestly. Continual suppression can lead to emotional turmoil, strained relationships, and even physical health issues. Like the beach ball, it's only a matter of time before suppressed emotions make their presence known, often in ways we didn't expect.

Numbness is not Healing

Pain, often seen as an enemy, naturally drives us to seek shelter, a form of self-preservation. However, in the refuge of avoidance, we unintentionally nurture our suffering. When grief knocks, we might divert our thoughts into activities, drown in busyness, or retreat into the haze of self-medication. Though momentarily relieving, these temporary exits are deceptive; **_numbness is not healing_**. By ignoring the pain, we merely silence the screams of our wounds, unseen beneath life's bandages, festering and deepening.

The consequences of repressed grief are far-reaching, extending beyond the present moment and potentially spiraling into depression, anxiety, or addiction. Healing demands the courage to embrace every emotional surge. The Grief to Growth Pathway is not a journey of erasing your pain, but one of transformation. It requires dismantling our walls, not to leave us defenseless, but to rebuild a stronger fortress within.

Letting in the storm of emotions is daunting, especially for those who steer their lives with control. It feels like uprooting stability. Yet, this deliberate step out of the numbness and into awareness is a decisive move toward growth. A participant in one of our group sessions shared her experience of embracing her emotions. She stated, "It is easy to stay busy, so I don't have to confront my emotions. But I am finding that when I slow down and embrace the awkwardness of my feelings, I learn so much about myself. I am not happy about my loss, but I can see the growth I am experiencing."

In this brave space of vulnerability, we genuinely process our emotions. But first, we must recognize and understand the common ways we numb ourselves to evade the very feelings that demand our attention:

Hyperactivity: Immersing ourselves in tasks, social events, or work to dodge solitude and silence where our thoughts get louder.

Substance use: Turning to alcohol, drugs, or even excessive medication, seeking chemical comfort to blur the harsh edges of reality.

Digital distraction: Losing hours in the digital world, whether through social media, video games, or endless streaming, to escape the present.

Emotional isolation: Intentionally detaching from friends and loved ones, creating physical and emotional barriers to avoid empathy or pity.

Overindulgence: Seeking refuge in food, shopping, or other forms of consumption to fill the void but creating fleeting highs followed by deep crashes.

Denial: Minimizing the gravity of our loss or change, pretending "everything is fine," masking our turmoil with false positivity.

Each of these shelters lures us with the promise of relief, yet each, in turn, distances us from healing. True growth stems from the willingness to cross the valleys of our grief, recognizing that the pathway out is through. I was listening to a podcast that featured a prominent entrepreneur. He talked about how he had been very successful, but the pressure to accomplish more accompanied that success. He dealt with anxiety and other health issues as a result. His breakthrough came when he understood he couldn't achieve his way out of it; he had to grieve his way through it. Emotions, however turbulent, are the guides we should seek to understand, not silence.

Understanding the Nuances of Loss

Loss manifests in many forms, and individuals experience and process grief uniquely. By understanding the variables involved and bringing compassion to your unique journey, you can healthily navigate grief and ultimately turn loss into growth. Losing a close loved one, especially a child, spouse, or sibling, often represents the most intimate loss, severing a significant emotional and physical bond between individuals. Losing a family member or friend to suicide adds layers of questioning, guilt, and trauma to the grieving process. Even if you expect the loss, grief still comes. Beyond death, many other losses can spur significant grief, including divorce or breakups, a complicated adoption process, job loss, infertility, estrangement, financial hardship, and loss of abilities through illness or aging.

Your faith, spiritual practices, and cultural traditions can provide an outlet for the collective processing of loss. Personal rituals also bring comfort. The depth of the relationship, the suddenness of the loss, past trauma, existing mental health challenges, and the availability of a support system shapes the grieving process. Depending on biology and socialization, men, women, and children process grief somewhat differently.

There is no perfect way to grieve. Be patient with yourself and honor your personal path. Let go of "I should have" and the expectations of predictable, linear stages. Grief brings raw, messy emotions. Allow them to flow, seeking support as needed.

Emotionally Processing Grief

In this chapter, we have seen that the emotional impact of grief is an unfolding process rather than a single challenge to clear. It requires a commitment to process the impact on our lives. We previously discussed the dangers of numbness. Now, let's look at ways we can actively take part in processing the various emotions.

Emotional Acknowledgement: Identifying and naming the emotions you are experiencing is a helpful process. Acknowledging these emotions, whether it be sadness, frustration, denial, or even a sense of relief, can liberate you from their silent control.

Expressing Grief: The expression of grief goes beyond creative outlets, encompassing a wide range of emotions. By externalizing your grief, you allow for an honest confrontation with your pain, a necessary step.

Seeking Support: Engage with friends, family, therapists, or support groups. These connections reaffirm you are not alone and provide a compassionate space to voice your struggles and victories.

Creating Rituals: Rituals, whether religious or personal, can offer comfort. Whether you light a candle, revisit cherished locations, or gather for remembrance events, these acts create a space where memories can be treasured and grief expressed.

Allowing Time: Recognize that time's passage offers a shift in perspective. The immediacy of pain reduces, making room for moments of unexpected joy and budding hope. Permit yourself to live in each emotion as time peels back layers of the grieving process.

Reframing Thoughts: Treasure positive memories and absorb the lessons these experiences have taught you. Considering how this transformative journey can lead to a new purpose can be helpful. Reframing allows you to reconstruct the loss as a waypoint rather than an end.

Rebuilding Routines: Gradually reintroduce structure into your life. The familiarity of daily routines offers a counterbalance to the chaos of grief. Yet, remember, this process is not about rushing back to "normal" but establishing a stabilizing rhythm in your new reality.

Physical Outlet: Engage in physical activities—be it walking, stretching, or more intensive exercise—that help dissipate the physical manifestation of your emotional turmoil. These actions are not escapes but therapeutic outlets for your grief.

Emotionally processing your grief is an active, deliberate journey. Through this, you transform your relationship with grief into a pillar of growth and resilience.

Painting Your Emotions

Imagine a canvas. When you think about the strokes that create a masterpiece, there are rarely straight lines. They're imperfect, they cross over, and sometimes, they're a complete mess. This chaos and lack of straight lines are a genuine reflection of our emotions during times of distress. A messiness seems to cloud our existence, and it often feels like we're losing control, reminiscent of an artist in the throes of creation.

In our interactive presentations, Kari and I introduce participants to 'pouring art,' a form of expression that harnesses this chaos. Here, you're not just applying paint but pouring your emotions out, allowing them to blend and merge on the canvas. This method, albeit uncontrollable at times, uses various colors to symbolize the spectrum of human emotions. During one memorable session, we witnessed the power of vulnerability. Participants opened up, revealing raw emotions - insecurity, guilt, rage, fear, loneliness, jealousy, feeling overwhelmed, and numbness. Each word and confession was a poignant acknowledgment of their internal struggles through grief.

We assigned a unique color to each emotion expressed, pouring the corresponding color of paint into a single cup. With every admission of guilt, a surge of dizziness, or confession of loneliness, we added a new hue, layering them in that container. What we created was a mosaic of colors, coming together to tell a story. After inverting this cup onto the canvas, the participants observed a calm containment of the paint. But as we continued our discussion, the paint began to seep out, each color inching its way beyond the confines, creating its path. Eventually, we lifted the cup to allow the paint to flow freely. Painting our emotions is not just an artistic exercise; it symbolizes the messiness and the beauty of human vulnerability. As the paint seeps, spreads, and eventually covers the canvas, it represents our journey through grief.

In our journey of The Grief to Growth Pathway, there comes a transformative moment of surrender. This moment is challenging for those of us who thrive on control, meticulously plan every aspect of our lives, and desperately hold the reins of our emotions, especially during the turmoil of grief. For my fellow 'control freaks,' the process of pouring art — of painting emotions — can initially feel unsettling, even frightening. We approach the canvas with a preconceived notion, a precisely imagined blueprint of where each color should flow and how the painting should look. We want the blue to streak across a specific corner, perhaps symbolizing a lingering sadness or melancholy we can't shake. But grief, with its unpredictable temperament, doesn't adhere to our plans. It hits unexpectedly, causing colors to run wild beyond the boundaries we attempt to set. This chaos, this loss of control, mirrors our life during periods of mourning. It's messy, it's untamed, and it's incredibly frustrating.

Herein lies an opportunity — the power to tilt the canvas. We cannot dictate how our emotions will mix or the courses they will take, but we can influence their direction. By tilting the canvas, we give our feelings permission to flow, perhaps for the first time. We're not surrendering to the chaos; we're directing it into something that, although still uncertain, can turn into a beautiful mosaic of our inner turmoil. With mindfulness, we guide these emotions, understanding that, like the streams of paint, they need to run their course.

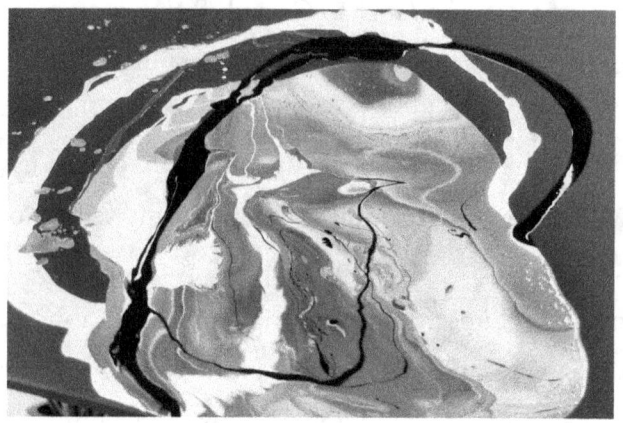

Embracing the overflow is an essential part of this healing. There will be instances when the paint — our emotions — dribbles over the edge, creating unexpected patterns and shapes... even a little mess. Emotions won't adhere to neat confines. They'll spill, they'll cause disorder, and they'll demand to be seen and felt. But it's in this overflow, this honest outpouring, where the true beauty of our human experience lies. By allowing our feelings space to exist

— unjudged, acknowledged, and respected — we're enabling the artwork of our soul to take shape.

As we step back and look at the canvas of our lives, it's easy to get overwhelmed by the chaotic blend of colors, the unanticipated patterns, and the uncertainty of what's emerging. However, in this chaos, a masterpiece is forming. It signifies our resilience and capacity to feel, heal, and grow.

So, when the control slips through your fingers, when the grief runs fresh, and when the canvas before you is unrecognizable — take heart. You're in the process of creating something genuinely remarkable. You're learning to find beauty in the brokenness, to see the emerging masterpiece within the mess. It's a testament to your strength, humanity, and the incredible blending of experiences that make up your life. Let the colors run; let the emotions flow. On the other side of this chaos, a unique, irreplaceable piece of art awaits — the renewed you.

The Art of Life

Following the loss of my wife, Jared Anderson, a friend and accomplished songwriter, invited me to stay at his home for a few days in Colorado Springs, Colorado. It was a refreshing time to process some of the previous year's events verbally. It was a lot to unpack from a cross-country move, Marybeth's cancer diagnosis, and then her passing within a year's time.

During that visit, we had breakfast at a local diner. We couldn't help but overhear the couple sitting next to us. This couple was trying to be civil with one another, but were discussing the details of their pending divorce. It was a sobering moment as we witnessed the hurt of others. As we returned to Jared's home, we started discussing the different struggles that we all face. Whether it be the loss of a loved one, the ending of a relationship, or even the pain of unrealized dreams.

Art of Life

Verse 1

A bend in the road so much I don't know
I won't make it on my own
I'm reaching to find a friend in the fight
Cause I'm losing control
And I can't say that I'm not afraid of the journey
They say carry on, but I need to be carried

Chorus

Through the night, One more step
Even if it's as far as I get
Would you stay by my side
As I pour out my heart into the Art of Life

Verse 2

Help me to make the most of these days
When the pain gets so hard
I can't catch my breath
Because I'm over the edge
Be my eyes in the dark
I'm trying to hold on, but it's hard to believe
I'm counting on faith, but there's no guarantee

Bridge

There's no straight lines on this canvas
It looks like a mess but it's not finished

Written by Jared Anderson & MattPerkins
One Side of the Righteousness/ASCAP (admin by Amplified Administration)
NuPraiz Publishing/ASCAP
Lyrics Used by permission

With its unforgiving timetable, life doesn't provide simple answers or painless shortcuts. The journey demands movement, even when every fiber of our being resists. While your loss journey may look different from ours, this revelation became the essence of "Art of Life," a song birthed from the agony, longing, vulnerability, and faint hope piercing through the thickest darkness.

"Art of Life" is more than a melody. It's a testament to our shared humanity, acknowledging that while the path is littered with obstacles, each step taken—even if it's a staggering jump—is a victory. The plea is simple: Surround yourself with others, share your story, and, in doing so, create a masterpiece from the pieces of our broken hearts. In this art of living, every color of paint, dark and bright, contributes to the canvas being beautifully transformed into a work of art.

At a Crossroads: The Power of Choice

Understanding and acknowledging the all-encompassing nature of loss is crucial. It's not just about the tangible absence of someone or something, but about the dreams, routines, roles, and potential futures that are altered or erased entirely. At some point, when navigating loss, we will stand at a crossroads. One path calls us toward suppression, a calm but ultimately stifling direction. Although more challenging, the other path urges us to confront and express, promising a journey of healing and understanding.

When grappling with loss, it's natural to encounter many emotions—some familiar, others foreign. This emotional crossroad can feel daunting. While it might seem tempting to choose the path of avoidance or denial, there's an innate power in facing our emotions head-on, giving them a voice and vocabulary.

Chapter 6

Paralysis

Processing Your Loss and Getting Unstuck

Near the equator lies a challenging zone where ships historically grappled with unpredictable or even absent winds. Sailors would remain stranded, without the wind's push, for days or weeks on end. This zone earned the name "the doldrums." The term later found its way into English, symbolizing periods of inactivity or stagnation.

Imagine a stifling summer in St. Louis, a place I recall from my Midwest upbringing. Anyone familiar with its humid summers would understand the oppressive weight of the air. One particular morning, my mom awoke to an overpowering stench. Glancing out her window, she saw a grim sight: dead fish floating atop the still waters of the neighborhood lake. The scorching heat, relentless humidity, and the lake's stillness had depleted its oxygen, rendering the water toxic. In such an environment, life could not persist. Similarly, when we become immobilized in our lives, trapped in a state of emotional uncertainty, we echo those stranded ships and that lifeless lake. Like being caught in the doldrums, we yearn for the winds of change or healing to propel us forward.

We have a tendency to seek order in chaos, and this inclination extends to the intense emotions we experience, such as grief. The temptation to set timetables and expectations for the grieving process is strong. You might think, "By this date, I should be past this," or "It's been a year; shouldn't I be over it by now?" However, grief defies such parameters. It is a unique journey for everyone, refusing to be boxed in or adhere to a preset schedule. While we wish there were a concrete path or an instant relief button, in reality there isn't one. Grief will take as long as it takes. It doesn't come with shortcuts or escape routes. The only way through it is to truly move through it.

In this chapter, we will explore the concept of grief paralysis, including its causes and symptoms. With this insight, you can learn to identify signs of being stuck or possibly even becoming codependent with your grief and empower yourself to move forward on your journey toward healing. With compassionate inner care, consistent effort, and the support of loved ones, you can transition your grief from a state of paralysis to active healing.

Navigating the Stagnant Waters

During paralysis, one often feels ensnared in a quagmire of emotions. It's as if the hands of time have frozen, and you're tethered to an inescapable dark realm. This stagnation isn't just an emotional state; it's a heavy weight pressing down on every thought and movement.

However, these waters, no matter how still, are not permanent. While you might feel encased in darkness, it is crucial to remember to reach out. A helping hand, be it a friend, family member, or professional, can be the breeze that helps navigate out of this standstill. It might seem daunting to make that call or share that feeling, but taking even the smallest action can start the journey out of this paralysis. And yes, people often liken grief to waves. There might be moments of calm where you feel the gentle ebb and flow of emotions, and suddenly, out of nowhere, you're blindsided by a tidal wave of sadness, anger, or despair. These abrupt surges can be disorienting, making the feeling of paralysis even more pronounced. It is in these overwhelming moments that a support system proves invaluable. They serve as the anchors, holding you steady as you brave the tumultuous waves.

Understanding Paralyzing Grief

Paralyzing grief, complicated grief, or prolonged grief disorder manifests when acute grief evolves into a chronic, debilitating condition. Those going through this type of grief often find themselves emotionally "stuck," unable to come to terms with their loss and progress in their healing journey. Instead of the typical grieving process, where the pain gradually lessens over time, paralyzing grief ensures that the person remains in a state of intense suffering.

Such a state of paralysis obstructs individuals from rediscovering a sense of purpose and meaning after their loss. Rather than adjusting to a new reality post-loss, these individuals remain anchored to the past, overwhelmed by sorrow, anger, or detachment. Even if they wish to move forward, they find themselves immobilized by constant anguish. Over time, this state exerts a significant psychological and physical strain.

Several factors can pave the way for the onset of grief paralysis. For instance, when death happens suddenly and unexpectedly, survivors miss out on anticipatory grieving, leaving them deeply shocked. Traumatic losses, like those stemming from suicide, homicide, or accidents, can lead to PTSD symptoms during the grieving process, manifesting as flashbacks, hypervigilance, or a sense of emotional numbness. Ambiguous losses, such as the disappearance of a loved one or situations like dementia, where the status of loss remains unclear, also hinder closure. Other contributing factors include a lack of social support, concurrent crises like a job loss or family conflict, and losses that evoke traumatic separations from childhood.

The unique circumstances of your loss, and your personal traits will shape how you grieve. While a temporary state of grief paralysis is a natural reaction immediately following a loss, therapeutic intervention becomes necessary when it persists.

Identifying the Signs of Being Stalled in Grief

If you constantly dwell on thoughts of your loss, yearn for what you no longer have, avoid activities or places associated with the deceased, or find yourself detached and emotionally numb, you might experience signs of being stalled in grief. Other indications include viewing life as empty without the departed, constantly plagued by images or thoughts of death, exhibiting irritability or bitterness, losing interest in social interactions, and feelings of confusion or suicidality. Suppose you blame yourself for the death or isolate yourself because of a lack of trust in others. In that case, it's essential to take note.

If you resonate with any of these experiences, grief may have you trapped. Left unaddressed, such intense and extended grieving can magnify pain, hinder healing, and lead to depression, post-traumatic stress disorder or PTSD, and other mental illnesses. Reaching out for professional guidance is imperative in these circumstances. Through their expertise, a counselor can offer coping techniques and treatment to assist you in moving through your grief. Remember, overcoming paralyzing grief is the key to discovering purpose and finding peace again.

The Risks of Co-Dependency

Grief has the power to transform us. When confronted with the pain of acute grief, the idea of ever experiencing joy can seem impossible. Our lives are sharply divided into the periods of "before" and "after" the incident, as the intense loss leaves an indelible mark. Yet, as time progresses, many bereaved individuals discover a "new normal." In this new phase, despite the lingering pain of loss, happiness can and often resurface.

However, there is a precarious edge where some individuals risk becoming deeply entwined with their grief. Instead of moving through their sorrow, they become inextricably bound to it. We often describe this situation as becoming "codependent" with one's grief. When someone is codependent with their grief, they might resist the idea of pursuing new interests or forming new relationships out of fear of betraying the memory of the deceased. They may operate under the belief that, without their grief, they are incomplete. For some, constantly reminiscing, crying, or viewing old photographs becomes a necessary ritual to feel close to the departed. Conversations and thoughts might revolve only around their loss, sidelining other aspects of their life.

This attachment can grow so much that the individual may feel overwhelmed with anxiety, panic, or despair if they are not actively grieving. Sometimes, they might use their grief as an excuse to evade responsibilities or inhibit their personal growth. Such an intense attachment to grief, this codependency, can act as a chain, binding us to our pain and obstructing the path to healing. It's an entanglement rooted in the fear of losing our grief because losing that grief might mean fully accepting the loss. Yet progressing through the thicket of sorrow is the only way to emerge on the other side where light, purpose, and renewed meaning await. Letting go of this codependency requires tremendous courage and commitment. Still, it is an essential step to growth and healing.

Getting Unstuck from Paralyzing Grief

When paralysis sets in, grief often makes us feel trapped in quicksand, unable to move or breathe. However, there are strategies that can help overcome this immobilizing sorrow. The initial step involves recognizing unhelpful patterns. Understanding and acknowledging behaviors or thought patterns that trap you in a cycle of grief is crucial. Ask yourself: which symptoms of complicated grief resonate with me? How might I be hindering my progress? Avoidance isn't the solution. Many people mistakenly believe that it will vanish if they ignore or suppress their grief. But the only path to healing is confronting that grief head-on. It requires courage to look squarely at your pain, to understand it, and to take proactive steps toward healing.

Another critical component is to express your emotions authentically. You're only deferring the pain when you bottle up feelings, especially intense ones like grief. Giving yourself the freedom to grieve that feels right to you is essential. This might mean allowing tears to flow unrestrainedly or channeling your pain into creative outlets like art. Ignoring or suppressing these emotions only sets the stage for a more tumultuous release later.

Last, don't underestimate the power of human connection. Grieving in isolation only magnifies the pain and hopelessness one feels. By reaching out—whether to trusted friends and family, a professional therapist, or a support group—you open yourself to the compassion and understanding that only others can provide. Sharing your story, raw and unfiltered, allows you to experience vulnerability and, in that space, find comfort and solace. Remember, as humans, we naturally incline towards connection, especially during times of deep sorrow, when we need a support network the most.

Support: Building Your Network

A supportive network is one powerful antidote to getting stuck in the grief process. While everyone's journey is unique, building and nurturing a support system can offer a lifeline of understanding, perspective, and encouragement. While many of us lean on friends and family in times of sorrow, it's essential to remember that the proper support isn't about quantity but quality. It's about finding individuals and communities who empathize with your pain and help you navigate your path to healing.

Family

Family acts as a double-edged sword. On one side, they share your grief and offer an understanding outsider can't provide. On the other side, familial ties bring complex emotions and expectations. Engage Openly, start conversations about your feelings and needs. It helps to set clear boundaries and ask for the specific support you want. And limit expectations, not every family member will understand or support your grief journey in the way you need. It's okay to seek understanding elsewhere.

Friends

Whether old or new, friends can play a crucial role in your support network. Their perspective, distanced from the immediate family dynamics, can often be refreshing. Diversify your friendship circle by surrounding yourself with a mix of friends—those who've experienced grief and can empathize, along with those who haven't but will listen and be there. Be sure to set boundaries. It's essential to communicate your needs and let friends know when their advice or presence may be more hindering than helpful.

Faith Community

For many, their faith community—whether a church, temple, or spiritual group — provides a foundation of hope and understanding. Seek solace in rituals. Many faiths have small groups or rituals around grief and loss. Engage in these to find both comfort and a sense of community. Connect with your Spiritual leaders who often have experience guiding individuals through grief. Their wisdom and perspective can be invaluable.

Support Groups

Support groups, whether formal therapy or informal meet-ups, can offer a space of mutual understanding and healing. Not every group will feel right. It's okay to visit a few until you find one where you feel at home. The more you put into the group, the more you'll get out. Share, listen, and connect.

Navigating Shifts in Your Inner Circle

As you rightly mentioned, our inner circle of support can evolve with the seasons of our grief journey. It's crucial to be adaptive and recognize when certain relationships are nurturing your growth and when they might stifle it. Recognize the intent but trust your journey. While loved ones may offer advice from a place of love, it's essential to recognize that their personal experiences or needs might influence their counsel. It's crucial to listen, but always trust your inner voice and pace in the grieving process. As you navigate your grief, seek those who align with your journey, even if they don't always agree with your methods or choices. Remember, grief is a very personal experience, and your pathway is uniquely yours. Building and nurturing the right support network can offer guidance, but always trust your heart and your journey.

Self-Compassion: Cultivating Your Soul

In the tempest of grief, pain, memories, and significant loss become the world's axis. However, even amidst this emotional tempest, one beacon steadfastly shines—self-compassion. This is not a nod towards pampering or indulgence but a pledge to your well-being, even amidst the chaos.

Demystifying Self-Compassion

Many misconceptions envelop the concept of self-compassion, particularly during the grieving process. Some perceive it as an act of selfishness, a deviation from the person or thing which was lost. Others interpret it as a signal of "moving on" too hastily or not grieving "appropriately." Let's dispel these myths: Self-compassion is not selfish. It is a discipline.

Why Discipline?

In this context, discipline signifies a deliberate and routine practice akin to brushing your teeth or consuming meals. You wouldn't forgo meals for days simply because you're grieving, right? Why? Because your body demands nourishment to function. Your heart and soul, much like your body, rely on self-compassion to heal and regain balance.

Pillars of Self-Compassion

Self-compassion, at its core, remains constant, but its implementation varies based on individuals' emotional, physical, and spiritual needs.

Physical

Rest: Healing occurs during rest. Even if grief disrupts sleep patterns, aim for regular sleep schedules and take naps when necessary.

Nutrition: Grief may suppress your appetite or trigger emotional eating. Attune to your body and supply balanced meals, fueling it with what it needs.

Exercise: Physical activity, even a mere walk outdoors, can release endorphins—natural mood enhancers. It has the dual benefit of protecting against depression and promoting mental clarity.

Emotional

Connection: While isolation might seem appealing, seek connection. Friends and family form a support network. They might not always comprehend your pain, but their presence can offer comfort.

Activities of Joy: Rekindling hobbies or discovering new ones can serve as a positive diversion and a means to channel your emotions.

Professional Support: Never hesitate to seek therapy or counseling. Mental health professionals provide coping tools and strategies and often furnish a safe space to express feelings.

Spiritual

Loss: Grief challenges our perspectives on faith and spiritual practices. Some might express anger or frustration towards God or spirituality. For others, spirituality becomes a source of strength and tranquility. This may involve prayer, meditation, or spending time in nature, providing solace and perspective.

How you choose to care for yourself during this journey is a deeply personal and introspective process. However, by acknowledging that self-compassion is a discipline, not a luxury, you empower yourself to heal and grow on your own terms.

Recognizing Emotional Triggers

Grief has a knack for catching us off-guard, sometimes turning simple daily activities into emotional roller coasters. How we navigate these moments determines whether we get stuck in our sorrow or gradually process and integrate our feelings. One way to ensure we stay on a path toward healing is by understanding and managing our emotional triggers. Perhaps you've found yourself caught off-guard by a song that brings memories flooding back or an unexpected scent that recalls shared moments with a loved one.

I remember wanting to make a special breakfast for my daughters after my wife passed away. I woke early and ran to the grocery store to get pancake ingredients. Knowing each daughter liked a specific syrup, I went down the aisle to get their preference. I looked over the different brands, and my mind suddenly locked up. How could I not remember which syrup each of them liked? I reached for my phone to text my wife... What was I thinking? I went from being eager to do something nice for my daughters to feeling guilty for not remembering a detail and being confused about trying to text my late wife. The tears started flowing as I left everything and went to my car. These triggers, as unexpected and heart-wrenching as they might be, are bridges to our past, reminding us of the depth of our bonds.

One of the major triggers that Kari experienced was driving in traffic behind an ambulance. Here is her story, and how she learned to manage this traumatic event.

On that Sunday, when Eddie died, we followed behind the ambulance, rushing him to the hospital. My head was a mess. Scared and confused, I was trying to figure out what had happened to Eddie.

And I was worrying about my kids, too. I had one of them with me, but the others were on their way to the hospital in different vehicles. I knew they were safe, but not knowing exactly where unsettled me. My phone kept ringing, breaking into my thoughts. People were calling, wanting to know what was happening, but I didn't have answers. Why were they calling now, at this horrible time? To this day, I can still see that ambulance right in front of me. For a while, whenever I would find myself behind an ambulance, those same anxious feelings would come rushing back. I remember the fear of the unknown, the worry for Eddie, and the frustration of that day. It's like it pulled me back in time, and I was there all over again.

So, how did I manage that trigger? I turned. I took a different street or turned as soon as possible. Turning away and taking a different path helped me feel somewhat in control. I was saying to myself, "It's okay, Kari. You're not stuck in that day." I knew I couldn't escape my memories, but taking a slight turn away from the ambulance helped me handle those big, scary feelings.

Though we can't predict every trigger that happens, knowing that they exist can help us. What I found helpful from Kari's experience was her response after she recognized the impact of an ambulance driving by... *"I turned."* Once we recognize that something is a trigger and the impact that it has on us, many times, we then have the ability to manage it. When something triggers feelings or experiences in your life, take a moment and journal about it. Write the circumstances, along with the feelings and emotions that were brought up. When we see this written in our own words, we can then process it more effectively.

Verbalizing our emotions can help us process and release them. Therefore, throughout this book, we emphasize having a strong support network. When we have others who understand loss, or will listen as you process your feelings, it can have a positive effect. If you don't have friends or family who you can verbally process your feelings with, I encourage you to find a support group. Besides processing your emotions with others, it is important to release self-blame when unexpected triggers arise.

Triggers are often associated with negative experiences surrounding loss. But while they may intensify our emotions, they can also highlight cherished memories we have shared. In the same way that a song can stir negative emotions, there are others that can be a source of comfort. Whether it stirred positive or negative feelings up, it's essential to embrace, understand, and know that you can manage these unpredictable waters.

Regardless of its source, grief offers a unique opportunity for personal evolution. Recognizing and managing our triggers allows us to maneuver through this journey with dignity, compassion, and wisdom. Though painful, in this path lies the potential for personal growth and rediscovering inner strength.

Beyond the Doldrums

Navigating the Paralysis phase, one may often feel trapped in the seemingly endless expanse of the Doldrums, where progress seems stagnant and emotions hover heavily. However, remember that just like a ship stranded in calm waters, with the right push and the right tools, you can find your way forward. Growth and healing aren't linear; there will be moments of despair, but equally, there will be moments of enlightenment and resurgence. Don't let grief become an immobilizing force. Instead, let it be a chapter that leads to beautiful stories of strength, resilience, and hope.

You have the strength within you to move beyond paralysis. Beware of the chains that grief might try to impose. Hold on to your memories, cherish them, and embrace the present and the future. Your journey from grief to growth is a testament to your spirit and the love you carry.

Chapter 7

Perspective

Seeing Loss in a New Light

Perspective is the lens through which we view our experiences, the prism that refracts the light of life into its myriad shades. This lens is often clouded during grief, casting shadows on our hearts and minds. But as the haze lifts, we find that perspective has the potential to illuminate even the darkest of areas, revealing paths we never imagined. When viewed through the proper lens, grief isn't just an experience of loss; it's a catalyst for unimaginable growth.

There's a grace in perspective. As we stand at the crossroads of despair and hope, it calls us to a transformative understanding. It's a gentle whisper reminding us that while the pain of loss is undeniable, it can also foreshadow a season of growth. It's not about masking the hurt or erasing memories but embracing every part of our experience... the pain, the messiness, the heartbreak, and the hope and growth awaiting us. Let me encourage you. Gaining perspective isn't about replacing what you lost or recreating past moments. It's about charting new territories of understanding and realizing that our grief is not an endpoint, but an intersection. It's where our experiences and future aspirations converge, where memories meet dreams, and where tears can be seeds for growth.

In the following pages, we explore the intricate layers of perspective. We will grasp how it can transform not only our perspective on our loss but also our perspective on ourselves and our role in this immense universe. By comprehending the significance of transitions and understanding their pivotal role in our journey, we establish the foundation for a life that acknowledges pain, but does not let it define us.

Understanding How You View Your Loss Impacts Your Healing

When confronted with loss, it can feel like the light has left your life. You may struggle to get through each moment in the early days and weeks after a traumatic loss. Heartache, anxiety, anger, or fear touches everything. Gaining any perspective apart from the pain may seem impossible. However, how you perceive and find meaning from your loss significantly impacts your healing capacity. While grief naturally brings acute suffering, how you view your experience is crucial in how fully and quickly you can process it.

> *"When we can no longer change a situation, we are challenged to change ourselves."*
>
> Viktor Frankl

Numerous studies have found that people who engaged in meaning-making after losing a loved one, such as reframing the loss or finding significance, showed better psychological change. Working to find or create meaning in your loss helps you gain perspective. This enables you to integrate the loss into the story of your life in a more positive, hopeful way. The process of gaining perspective does not always occur quickly or easily. Be patient and gracious with yourself, acknowledging that shifting your viewpoint takes time and concentrated effort. But know that reaching a place of deeper understanding and peace regarding your loss is possible.

> *"Meaning-making can help you rise above what is beyond your control and transform fears into faith, trust, altruism, and courage."*
>
> Dr. Paul Wong

Changing the Lens

When discussing perspective and seeing your loss in a new light, we are not implying that you should convince yourself that the loss was a good thing. And when others encourage you to gain perspective or "look on the bright side" of your loss, it can come across as insensitive, unrealistic, or even offensive. You may feel that taking any viewpoint other than grief means denying the tragedy, minimizing your pain, or harboring false hope. However, a shifting perspective does not require any of these things.

Perspective simply means looking at a situation through a particular lens or viewpoint. Consider how a photographer will use different lenses to adapt to various conditions and also to express their vision most effectively. With each lens change, there are new opportunities and challenges to capture a compelling image. After a significant loss, you naturally view your circumstances primarily through the lens of grief, sorrow, fear, or anger—and rightfully so. However, you can also learn to shift into other beneficial perspectives that do not negate or override your grief, but help balance it. For instance, you might search for deeper understanding by reflecting on how the loss has influenced your essence or reshaped your priorities. By immersing yourself in the treasured memories shared with your loved one, you can cultivate an enriched sense of appreciation. There's also the opportunity to nurture hope, rooted in the belief that you possess the inner fortitude to chart a way forward.

Think of these new perspectives as additional lenses to view through, rather than a substitute for the lens of grief. Sometimes, you may peer through the meaning lens, gaining comfort as you assemble the fragmented pieces of your loss into a coherent narrative. At other times, the appreciation lens will enable you to focus on the blessing of past joy rather than just present and future pain. The grief lens will probably remain dominant for some time—and this is appropriate. But occasionally, viewing your loss through lenses of meaning, hope, shared experience, or growth will provide balance, comfort, and an expanded capacity to heal. Think of shifting perspective not as false hope but as gaining a complete, truthful understanding of your multifaceted experience.

Ultimately, the key word in all of this is "change." Even in the best of situations, change is hard. This is one of the most challenging parts of grief. Understanding transitions and how to move through them gracefully is critical.

Why Transitions Matter

In life, just as in music, transitions act as bridges, guiding us from one state or place to another. Imagine navigating through a song: the bridge uniquely carries both the lyrics and melody to a distinct and different place. This bridge builds momentum as it approaches the next chorus. This transformative section demands the listener's attention, preparing them for a powerful return with greater impact. Now, relate this metaphor to life's transitions: when everything feels distinct, slightly offbeat, and out of time, consider this your life's bridge. This vital, although uncomfortable, transition period sets the stage, preparing you to emerge into the next chapter. This is your personal, impactful chorus - with new strength and perspective. Embrace the shift, for it crafts the path leading toward growth.

Transitions are the inner processes or periods of change as we let go of old realities and learn to embrace new ones. They involve fundamental shifts in our identities, relationships, behaviors, and sources of meaning. Dr. William Bridges, a leader in transition studies, stated that transition "is the psychological process of adapting to change."[1] Change happens externally, but transition occurs internally.

"Not in his goals, but in his transitions, man is great."
Ralph Waldo Emerson

Types of Transitions in Grief

Several types of transitions typically occur when you experience a significant loss. Understanding the core transitions can help you

---

1. Bridges, W. (1980). Transitions: Making Sense of Life's Changes. Addison-Wesley.

name your experiences, feel less alone, and gain perspective on navigating change. Common grief-related transitions include:

Relational transitions - The loss markedly changed your relationships. For example, losing a spouse transforms familial roles and dynamics with children and others.

Identity transitions - A significant part of your identity is now missing, forcing the reformulation of your self-concept. For instance, losing a career-defining job requires rethinking your professional identity.

Meaning transitions - When you lose something that gave your life significance and purpose, you must find new meaning. For example, losing a child could eliminate a key source of meaning as a parent.

Health transitions - The loss impacts your physical or mental wellness, causing lifestyle adjustments to regain health. For instance, extreme grief may require medication, therapy, rest, or other care.

Emotional transitions - You must learn to regulate your emotions in new ways as you process the many feelings of grief. Identifying and managing swirling, often intense emotions becomes crucial.

Financial transitions - Certain losses bring major financial changes, such as losing a spouse who was the primary breadwinner. Adjusting budgets and finances becomes essential.

You can gain a helpful perspective by identifying the transitions you are navigating. You can research how to best cope with that type of transition and find encouragement through others' insights and experiences. Naming your transitions acknowledges the hard inner work you are doing in this season. This process takes time, but ultimately empowers transformation.

Coping with the Challenges of Transitions

Navigating fundamental life transitions requires an immense amount of work. To be completely honest...it's draining. You may feel overwhelmed and under-equipped. Give yourself the grace to move through changes slowly. Attend to your physical and mental well-being. Do the emotional and spiritual work necessary to process the old and embrace the new. Remember that transitions are a normal part of life's journey. While difficult, you will get through this process if you are patient, get adequate support, and trust your inner resilience.

Grief as a Transition

At its core, grief is transition. You can't go back to what was, and it's too painful to stay where you are. We have to find a path forward. When we see this grief journey as a transition, it can provide a helpful perspective. Rather than just a period of painful chaos to survive, you can view grief as an impactful transition guiding you toward transformation and growth. This transition perspective highlights that, like other life transitions, grief holds the potential for growth, learning, and developing new inner strengths and resources. It normalizes the challenging emotions you must work through as you transition. Viewing grief as a transition provides hope that you can actively move through the painful inner work and come out the other side stronger.

The Power of Moving Forward Versus Moving On

A key concept to understand when coping with loss is the vital difference between moving forward versus moving on. In the early shock of grief, you may vacillate between feeling completely stuck and wanting to escape the painful reality of your loss altogether. However, neither of these responses promotes healing. There is a vital difference between "moving forward" versus "moving on." It may sound like we are making a big deal out of words to some. They say, "Relax, it's just semantics. They mean the same thing." For Kari and me, we cringe whenever someone comments, "It looks like you've moved on." But, we didn't *move on* from our grief... we are intentionally *moving forward* with it. Let's look further at some key differences in the use of these terms.

Moving On

Moving on promotes leaving grief behind entirely to forget the pain and pretend life is the same as before the loss. In our fast-paced society, we naturally seek the fastest way to accomplish a task and move on to the next one. However, an achievement-based mindset can cause issues in the context of significant life transitions. Rather than swift and predictable, grief is a prolonged process of incorporating loss into one's life.

Moving Forward

Moving forward, however, means intertwining the past and the present, cherishing the memory of your loved one while living fully in the moment. It involves creating new routines, pursuing new interests, and honoring the one you lost through legacy projects, or sharing positive memories. With each intentional step, you can feel a sense of empowerment as you uncover new meaning and purpose. It makes space for grief while also embracing opportunities for joy and meaning. Progress gradually comes through feeling all the complex emotions of grief and navigating associated transitions while also looking toward the horizon of hope.

Growth Versus Replacing Loss

Another critical perspective shift to make in grief is understanding the difference between personal growth and replacing loss. Healing from loss occurs through grief work, affirming memories, discovering meaning, and gradual growth. We do not achieve growth by attempting to replace what you lost quickly. Growth after a loss can involve learning new skills, deepening spirituality, spending quality time with other loved ones, focusing on physical or mental health, pursuing meaningful causes, or embracing life's small joys with more gratitude. Growth directs energy toward your inner life and existing relationships.

Replacing, conversely, tries to substitute someone or something for your loss through quick fixes like leaping into new relationships, buying material items, moving locations abruptly, or making rash life changes. Replacing distracts from inner work by focusing energy externally.

In early grief, replacing may temporarily numb the pain. But it ultimately stunts healing and growth. The perspective to embrace is that no person or thing can fully replace what you lost. Each loss is unique. However, as you move forward, you can discover additional sources of meaning, joy, and purpose. Your grief journey will involve gradual growth, not replacement. Activities like journaling, therapy, long nature walks, or loving support from friends who allow you to express emotions can help facilitate helpful growth. Look for opportunities to expand your capacities for compassion, wisdom, strength, and hope. Be the soil where growth can take root even as you grieve what you lost.

Perspective Shapes Your Path

How you perceive or find meaning from your loss will greatly shape your path. Gaining helpful perspectives is not about denial or false hope. It is about utilizing lenses of possibility—meaning, hope, or growth—to balance the pain that naturally results from trauma. Consider perspective a series of gentle pivots. The pivot from only painful emotions to also remembering joy. A shift from feeling stuck to taking small steps forward. A change from panic to calm awareness. You restructure the questions from "Why?" to asking, "How can this shape me?" These pivots toward new perspectives emerge gradually through inner work and support. Your loss has forever changed your world. But your perception, shaped by new perspectives, can forever change your capacity to heal.

"We suffer more in imagination than in reality."
Lucius Annaeus Seneca

The way you imagine your loss and grief journey possesses immense power. When I was in high school, I remember walking through the mall during the holiday season, and the popular items that stores would sell were 3D posters. At first glance, you would see one image. But the longer you looked at it, another image would emerge that was three-dimensional. Gaining perspective isn't just about looking at a situation from a different angle, but having the patience to allow something new to emerge. Allowing your perspective to shift and expand will enable you to breathe, grow, and eventually dance again, even in a different rhythm.

Seeing Loss as a Catalyst for Growth

Loss slices life irreversibly into pieces that we cannot repair or fully restore. It is impossible to bring back or replace the person or thing taken from you. However, the loss can also be a powerful catalyst for growth and positive transformation in your life. The key lies in shifting your perspective to seek opportunities amid grief rather than staying trapped in suffering. Viktor Frankl, a renowned psychiatrist and Holocaust survivor wrote extensively about using suffering as a catalyst. He said, "In some ways, suffering ceases to be suffering at the moment it finds a meaning... Therefore, it is not the experience of today that drives people mad - but the remorse over something that happened yesterday and the dread of what tomorrow might bring."[2]

By perceiving loss as an opportunity for growth and transformation instead of devastation, your perspective shifts. From the rubble, you can start rebuilding your life in meaningful new ways that honor the past and present. Seeing loss as a growth catalyst empowers you to make the most of your suffering. Frankl called this "pulling meaning out of suffering" and considered it vital to overcoming adversity. Of course, you cannot force personal growth, which will occur gradually. But the perspective shift

---

2. Frankl, V. E. (2006). Man's Search for Meaning. Beacon Press. (Original work published 1946)

from "this loss destroyed me" to "this loss can transform me" is significant.

You move beyond victimhood when you see yourself as an active participant in your journey. You ask empowering questions, such as "How can this loss shape me into someone new? What purpose or meaning can I find in my remaining years? How can I use my experiences to help others?" Seeing loss through the lens of growth places you in the driver's seat, oriented toward the horizon ahead.

Importance of Community Support

One of the most vital resources for gaining perspective during grief is other people. Loss can easily isolate you. Connecting with others who understand your sorrow helps you see things you cannot alone. Support groups, grief counseling, talking with wise friends—community provides mirrors to show blind spots and compassion to soothe wounds.

Do not isolate yourself. There is perspective, empathy, and even laughter in those who understand the trenches of pain and growth you are navigating. In his book, *The Four Loves*, C.S. Lewis said, "Friendship is born when one person says to another: 'What! You too? I thought I was the only one.'"[3]

Practical Strategies for Gaining Perspective

Perspective evolves gradually as you actively navigate the inner terrain of grief. Small, daily choices to engage in practices that shift your perspective make a difference. Consider incorporating some of the following strategies:

Journal: Write about parts of your loss story and moments of hope, meaning, or beauty you observe daily.

Express gratitude: Notice and give thanks for even tiny blessings each day, training your mind away from loss.

Help others: Get involved with a cause or organization related to your loss to help others navigate similar grief.

Celebrate legacy: Share positive memories and carry on traditions or activities your lost loved one enjoyed. This brings perspective on how they still impact you and others.

Share feelings: Be open and vulnerable with trusted friends about your complex emotions and experiences. Verbalizing provides relief.

Pursue new interests: Exploring new hobbies or activities that fascinate you helps you focus outward and find joy.

Get outdoors: Spend time walking or sitting in nature. Nature's beauty and constancy provide perspective.

Read books on grief: Build your knowledge and find connections with those who have walked the path before you.

Talk to a counselor: Professional help provides tools to process trauma and gain insights you cannot alone.

Perspective evolves slowly out of daily intention. Commit to small choices grounded in community, inner-care, learning, and meaning-making. Like a mosaic, each piece eventually forms a new picture of loss, different from the broken fragments at the start of grief. You will get through this and discover just how strong and wise you can become.

The Power of Reframing Loss

Learning to reframe your loss is one of the most essential perspective shifts you can make in grief. Reframing means taking a situation and intentionally looking at it through a different interpretive lens. Reframing loss empowers you to find new meaning and possibility amid tragedy. Of course, the losses themselves were horrible and unfair. However, the grief-stricken individuals intentionally reframed the tragedies as catalysts rather than destroyers. This allowed them to discover hope, meaning, community, new skills, and an ongoing bond with what they lost.

Reframing takes time, intention, and often support from others to gain new perspectives. Gradually, moments of meaning and even gratitude emerge when you purposefully shift your inner lens. The pain of loss endures, yet reframing presents the opportunity to reconstruct and find wholeness.

Intention and Purpose

Gaining perspective in grief allows you to move forward with renewed intention, purpose, and meaning. Rather than remaining stuck in your pain or fruitlessly rushing to "get over it," you can walk a thoughtful path of integration. Your loss will remain part of you, as it should. It has become part of what shapes your days from this point onward. However, you get to choose how you view the loss each day and what meaning you make from the experience.

The process of advancing after experiencing loss can be a complex and deeply personal journey. It often requires integrating deliberate actions and intentions into one's daily life. Each day, consider taking tangible steps that offer you a sense of purpose and progress. This doesn't mean grand gestures; sometimes, it's the small, meaningful goals that make all the difference. It could be a commitment to emotional well-being, nurturing relationships, starting new activities, or even doing something special in honor of your loved one's memory.

It's crucial to give yourself the grace to grieve, but it's equally essential to strike a balance. Ensure that amidst the grieving, you carve out time for rest, to experience joy, and to embrace life to its fullest. Maintaining this balance helps to avoid being completely consumed by grief. Connection is vital. Find practices that keep the bond with your lost loved one alive. For some, it may involve revisiting old photographs, recreating their favorite dishes, or taking trips to places that held meaning for them. Such acts can provide comfort during difficult moments. Consider becoming involved in support groups or activities that align with your type of loss. Engaging with others who've experienced a similar tragedy can provide both solace and a new perspective. It can also be a way to make meaning out of your pain as you aid others on their journey through grief.

Even in the darkest moments, it's imperative to hold on to hope. Embrace the light that represents hope, inner strength, love, gratitude, or a brighter tomorrow. No matter how dark it gets, there's always some light around; all it takes is the courage to look for it. This path of grief often feels lonely and aimless. But by gaining perspective, you can move forward with renewed intentionality in how loss will shape the rest of your days. You have power over the meaning you make each moment. As Viktor Frankl said, "Everything can be taken from a man but one thing: the last of the human freedoms—to choose one's attitude in any given set of circumstances." Choose perspective, choose purpose, choose hope.

Grief brings crushing darkness. Yet, as you learn to shift perspective, glimmers of light appear that illuminate a way forward. You will never see the loss in the same way again—the naivety of wholeness is gone. But through reframing loss and seeking meaning, you gain a new vision. As painful as grief is, know that this loss also shapes you. Let it forge unbreakable strength, deepen relationships, refine your purpose, develop compassion, and unveil hidden wells of wisdom within you. You now have tools to help you move forward with intention into a life that integrates loss but holds even more significant meaning.

Chapter 8

Purpose

Dreaming For What Is Next

"You don't have to have it all figured out to move forward."

This statement reverberates with truth. The notion that we need to have everything in place before we can take a step is not just limiting, but also unrealistic. Life, with its unpredictable ebb and flow, seldom works in a linear or predetermined way. Often, the challenges, like a significant loss, shake the foundation of our existence and urge us to reevaluate our path and purpose.

When faced with the undeniable realities of 'what was,' it's easy to get caught up in the whirlpool of memories, longing, and emotions. This isn't just about remembering the past, but also recognizing its deep impact on your current self. How has your loss shaped you? Have you discovered new facets of your being? Maybe resilience you didn't know you had? These questions act as anchors, helping you understand where you've been and, equally important, where you might head.

Yet, as you stand in the 'what is,' you might grapple with various emotions. The stark realities of your current situation, be it caring for a loved one with a diminished capacity, facing financial or health challenges, or realizing that your previous plans or perspectives no longer align with your newfound truths, can be daunting. While sometimes harsh, this present is your compass, directing you toward 'what's next.' Remember, just because your life doesn't mirror the picture you once imagined doesn't mean it's any less meaningful.

It's all too easy to revert to what's familiar when faced with uncertainties. We crave stability and a sense of normality, especially after a significant upheaval. However, it's crucial to recognize that chasing after what was can deter the possibilities of what could be. Jumping back into old habits or rushing into situations to feel a semblance of your old normal might offer temporary comfort. Still, true healing and growth come from acknowledging and facing change head-on.

The difficult space in which you stand, bridging your past and present, holds potential. Here, dreams take shape, visions form, and hope reignites. Dreaming of 'what is next' is about reimagining what happiness, success, and fulfillment look like for you now. Your dreams and aspirations might look different post-loss, and that's okay. The beauty lies in the journey of rediscovery and the chance to mold a life that resonates with your evolved self.

This chapter will guide you as you navigate the sometimes murky waters of grief, loss, and the eventual resurgence of hope and purpose. With every line you read and every insight you glean, remember that the strength to move forward doesn't come from having all the answers, but from the courage to ask the right questions and the willingness to embrace change. While it might differ from what you envisioned, your future can still hold beauty, growth, and newfound purpose.

Acknowledging What Was: An Essential Step in Healing and Growth

Life, with its myriad experiences, brings a spectrum of emotions. Moments of loss and grief invariably interweave with joy and happiness. While we all aspire to look forward and envision a brighter tomorrow, the journey ahead often requires us to pause, reflect, and embrace our past, particularly the losses that have punctuated our narratives.

The days leading up to what would have been my 30th wedding anniversary with Marybeth were heavy with significance. For many, there's an inclination to let such milestones fade or, worse, to suppress them, as if the past was a shadow best left unacknowledged. Kari was mindful of this date and said, "Matt, we have reservations for dinner tomorrow night to celebrate your anniversary." The thoughtfulness of that gesture was very impactful. Kari was mindful that the past is not a burden to carry, but a foundation upon which to build. Life constantly introduces additional elements: relationships, careers, and adventures. But these new chapters don't necessitate erasing what came before. Instead, we can integrate our experiences and memories into our evolving story.

I find it humorous to watch the puzzled look on people's faces when they come into my office for the first time. They seem very confused if they are unaware of our family's journey. When they see the pictures on the wall, they find a collage of pictures of Kari and Eddie with their boys, Marybeth, me, and the girls, and then photos of our wedding and blended family. I always laugh when they turn back to me with puzzled looks. That is one of the favorite displays in my office because it tells a story without words. My encouragement to you is that your past deserves to be celebrated. As you do, it can pave the path ahead with hope and confidence.

Be it a holiday celebration, the birth of a new family member, or another momentous occasion, these are reminders of a life richly lived. Sometimes, the memories they invoke are tinged with sadness, but they're often infused with joy and gratitude. Regardless of the loss that you have experienced, it's crucial to honor and celebrate what brought you to this point. If moments of pain arise, recognize the resilience and strength propelling you to the present. Remember, you have the power to step confidently into your future.

Why Acknowledging "What Was" Matters

Loss, in any form, carves an indelible void in our lives. Beyond the tangible absence, the emotional and psychological imprint remains. To truly heal and grow from such experiences, we must acknowledge them for two fundamental reasons:

For Healing: It provides an avenue to navigate our feelings, ultimately enabling us to heal and progress.

For Growth: It allows introspection, helping us discern how our experiences have molded us.

Honoring the Past

But how does one acknowledge and make peace with 'what was'? Here's a roadmap:

Tangible Memorials: Create dedicated spaces, memory books, or boxes that house photographs, letters, or belongings. These are bridges to the past, allowing you to journey back and cherish moments.

Commemorative Activities: Attend memorial services, volunteer for causes, donate, or join support groups. It keeps the essence of your loved one or the lost thing alive and offers a comforting sense of continuity.

Share Your Story: Journaling or conversing about your feelings and memories can offer relief. It externalizes your internal journey, making it tangible and easier to process.

Symbolic Continuation: Engage in activities that connect you with the essence of your loss. Play music, cook food, or pursue hobbies that are associated with the memory to create a spiritual and emotional bridge.

Accept Your Emotions: Grief is complex and multifaceted. Allow yourself to feel, whether it's pain, anger, guilt, or nostalgia, without judgment.

Reflect on its Influence: Consider how this loss influenced you. There's power in finding meaning in its role in your larger life story.

Your Unique Pace

Remember, grief doesn't follow a prescribed timeline. You undertake an individual journey. While you must make space for mourning, you also ensure that it doesn't trap you indefinitely.

When you honor and acknowledge 'what was,' you carve a path to cherish its memories and pave the way for 'what's next.'

Embrace What Is: The New Reality After Loss

Life after a significant loss can feel like a maze of emotions, challenges, and confusion. However, moving forward requires us to acknowledge and embrace our present circumstances—no matter how different or painful they might seem compared to our past.

Understanding the Present

In the aftermath of loss, it's easy to become enmeshed in memories and longing for what once was. While it's essential to honor these feelings, it's equally crucial to recognize and come to terms with the reality of the present. The world keeps turning, even if we feel we've reached a standstill.

Overcoming Denial and Avoidance:

Many of us experience denial after a significant loss. This protective mechanism can be helpful initially, providing a cushion from the sheer intensity of pain. But over time, avoiding our current reality hinders growth and adaptation. We must confront and adapt to the present rather than shy away from the present.

Strategies to Embrace the Now:

Discovering Joy Amidst Grief: It's okay to feel the sadness and the weight of your loss. Yet, even in moments of despair, seek those brief instances of happiness, gratitude, or purpose.

Honest Reflection: Take a compassionate look at where you are. Understand your needs, strengths, and where you might need support.

Adaptation: Your routines need to change. Rather than holding onto the past, craft new rituals that recognize and honor your current situation.

Inner-Care: Grief doesn't have a linear path. As you navigate its unpredictable path, prioritize inner-care and stress management.

Acknowledge Your Strength: Remember the times you've overcome challenges before this. Use tools and strategies that have helped you in the past.

Stay Connected: Grief can be isolating, but it's vital to maintain open communication with loved ones. Share your evolving feelings and needs.

Acceptance: Closure is a complex concept, and sometimes, it's elusive. Understand that even if you don't find complete closure, you can still adapt, grow, and lead a fulfilled life.

Permission to Thrive: As time passes, allow yourself to experience happiness without guilt. Envision your loved ones cheering you on, wanting the best for you.

Moving Forward with Wisdom and Gratitude:

Navigating through the landscape of loss and rebuilding isn't about severing ties with the past or diminishing the pain we've undergone. It's a transformative process, a redefinition of self that involves weaving the essence of what we've lost with what remains and is yet to come. This journey demands the bravery to stand firm in the now, recognizing its difference from our past and its potential for our future. It's here, in the heart of this awareness, that wisdom and gratitude find fertile ground.

In our family, we are mindful that not only Kari and I are processing grief. In the final chapter of this book, you will hear the stories of each of our kids. It was humbling to hear them articulate their journeys through grief, their struggles, and the personal victories they've achieved. Our daughter Alyssa's story strikes a resonant chord on the power of gratitude. Her recounting of how her mother's habit of daily gratitude journaling, inspired by Ann Voskamp's "One Thousand Gifts," deeply influenced her coping mechanisms. Alyssa's adaptation of this practice underscores a fundamental truth: gratitude doesn't always require a pen and journal, but a consistent acknowledgment—a mental note or whispered thank you—that can equally tether us to the present and counterbalance our loss.

"I may not put pen to paper as Mom did," Alyssa reflected, "but I have embraced her legacy of gratitude into my daily life. Each day, I try to make it a point to acknowledge the blessings around me, no matter how small. It's a tribute to her, a reminder that even in the trials, there are sparks of beauty worthy of our thanks." This practice, simple yet sincere, serves a dual purpose. First, it's a silent dialogue with the past, a way of carrying forward a loved one's legacy that intertwines with our personal growth. Second, it's an anchor, grounding us in the 'now' by compelling us to recognize the good surrounding us, even when clouded by grief. It is a reaffirmation of life and a testament to the resilience of the human spirit.

Embracing this mindset doesn't nullify the pain or negate the past. Instead, it fosters a healing environment where gratitude and memory walk hand in hand, bridging the past's sorrow and the present's potential for joy. It's a conscious choice, a daily practice, and perhaps most importantly, a tribute to the ones we continue to love and the continuous cycle of growth and gratitude they've inspired.

Dreaming for What Is Next

Every individual experiences a unique journey of grief and healing. Kari and I have faced the challenge of envisioning a future after loss, where dreams might feel distant or even impossible. However, understanding that the process, while complicated, also testifies to the resilience of the human spirit is essential. Let's look deeper into the process of dreaming for "what is next" and understand the hope it offers:

Embracing Micro-dreams: It's perfectly okay to start small. It might be as simple as taking up a new hobby, joining a book club, or making time for a weekly walk in nature. These micro-dreams can become your stepping stones to a bigger vision.

Guided by Your Core: As you journey through life, your core values and identity remain your compass. These intrinsic qualities will lead you, providing clarity in uncertain times.

Rediscover and Explore: Reconnect with the passions you once had or explore entirely new ones. Remember, it's a journey of discovery, not perfection.

Concrete Your Dreams: A vision board or a journal can be powerful tools to visualize your dreams. Sharing your aspirations with trusted loved ones can also make them more tangible, providing a sense of accountability and encouragement.

Growth in Adversity: Grief, though painful, can also be a catalyst for personal growth. Use this period to invest in yourself, whether it's through therapy, joining communities, or gaining new skills.

The Evolution of Dreams: Understand that as you evolve, so will your dreams. What you desire now might change in the future. This adaptability is a sign of growth and self-awareness.

Affirmative Mindset: Self-talk shapes our realities. Equip yourself with affirmations that reiterate hope, courage, and resilience. Challenge negative thoughts and let positivity guide you.

Though the future can sometimes appear overwhelming, especially after experiencing a loss, it's essential to remember that dreams aren't just figments of our imagination but seeds of hope. As you journey through your unique healing process, embrace the beautiful possibilities. The next chapter in your life story holds untapped potential and dreams yet to be discovered. The road might wind, but you'll find your way with courage and determination. Embrace your dreams, for they light your path forward.

Risk Tolerance: The Impact of Loss on Decision-Making

Experiencing a significant loss—whether it's the death of a loved one, deteriorating health, the end of a relationship, or a career setback—can greatly influence our perceptions, emotions, and behaviors. One notable change people often encounter, though not immediately recognized, is a shift in their tolerance for risk. Suddenly, once confident decision-makers may become hesitant and cautious, second-guessing even the smallest choices. Personally, I have found this to be true in my life. After losing my wife, I questioned my ability to make simple decisions, both personally and professionally. I didn't make the connection that this resulted from loss. But why does this change occur? Several emotional factors contribute to this.

Heightened Sense of Vulnerability

In its many forms, loss can peel back the layers of our emotional armor, exposing our raw and tender vulnerabilities. This heightened sensitivity can make the world seem more unpredictable and dangerous. We naturally want to protect ourselves from further harm when we feel vulnerable. Shattered assumptions also contribute to this sense of vulnerability. We might have believed the world to be safe, but a sudden loss can shatter that perception, making everything seem unpredictable. Loss has a way of challenging our beliefs and assumptions about the world and our place in it. It is natural to want to protect ourselves. This protective instinct can manifest in various ways, heightening our sense of vulnerability.

Loss of Confidence

Navigating grief often leads to a loss of confidence. Experiencing a significant loss can shake our trust in our judgment. As we grapple with the pain, we might question whether our past decisions played a role in the event, even when there's no direct connection. This self-doubt doesn't remain isolated; it infiltrates various facets of our lives.

This loss of confidence in the workplace can manifest as hesitation in deciding or doubting our professional capabilities. In relationships, we might second-guess our choices, wonder if we're worthy of love, or question our ability to maintain meaningful connections. Our self-esteem also takes a hit, leading us to undervalue ourselves and our contributions. As a result, we become less confident in personally and professionally assessing and managing risks.

Emotional Overwhelm

Grief can be all-consuming. When we experience feelings of sadness, anger, or guilt, they can consume our emotional bandwidth, leaving less cognitive space for analytical thought. The mental fog of grief can make even simple decisions seem overwhelming, leading many to avoid decision-making altogether, especially when risks are involved.

Fear of Compounding Loss

After you've experienced a significant loss, it's common to become hyper-aware of other potential losses that might lurk around the corner. The mere thought of risking something else, whether money, relationships, or opportunities, can feel overwhelming and paralyzing. This fear usually comes from the belief that you may not be capable of dealing with additional pain or disappointment.

Change in Priorities

Loss can shift our priorities. Things that seemed important before may seem trivial after a significant loss, leading to a change in how we evaluate risks. A once career-driven person may become risk averse in professional settings after the death of a loved one, prioritizing family and personal well-being over advancement or financial gain.

Seeking Stability

There's often an overwhelming desire for stability and predictability in the wake of a loss. Risks inherently involve the unknown, and after a loss, many individuals crave the comfort of the familiar and predictable. Taking risks may feel like inviting additional chaos into an already rough emotional landscape.

Physical and Mental Exhaustion

Grief isn't just an emotional process; it can be physically and mentally draining. When exhausted, our capacity to assess and take on risks diminishes. Decision fatigue sets in, making even minor choices seem daunting.

Navigating Risk Post-Loss

Understanding these factors is crucial, especially for individuals navigating the grief process and for those supporting them. Realizing that feeling less inclined to take risks is a common reaction to encountering loss can lay the groundwork for self-compassion and patience.

However, it's also essential to find a balance. While being more cautious after experiencing loss is okay, avoiding risks can lead to missed opportunities and hinder personal growth. With the proper guidance, individuals can learn to acknowledge their fears and vulnerabilities while taking measured steps toward regaining confidence and re-establishing risk tolerance. Finding a new equilibrium after loss is possible through patience, understanding, and targeted strategies.

The Power of Resilience: Setting the Stage for Your Next Chapter

Resilience isn't just about bouncing back; it's about moving forward with a deeper understanding, grace, and an enlightened perspective. Life is a series of ever-turning pages and chapters filled with joys, sorrows, and revelations. But what happens when one of those chapters is so challenging that moving forward seems impossible? It's in these moments of deep despair and hardship that our resilience shines brightest. For you, resilience in grief means allowing yourself to feel the depth of your pain without being consumed, looking ahead with hope without negating your past.

It's Not About Denying Emotions

In our society, there's a prevalent misconception about resilience. Many believe that to be resilient, one must suppress emotions, especially those deemed "negative" or "weak." This couldn't be further from the truth. Phrases like "Stay strong" or "Don't cry" are often well-intentioned. They come from a place of wanting to protect or shield someone from pain. However, they can inadvertently convey that feeling pain or sorrow is a sign of weakness. This can lead to internalized guilt or shame about natural emotional responses.

True resilience is not about avoiding the storm but learning to dance in the rain. It's about recognizing that emotions, whether joy or sorrow, are a natural part of the human experience. When we fully experience our emotions, we gain insight into our identity and our perception of the world. When we give ourselves the grace to cry, we are not showing weakness but wisdom and strength. It takes courage to face our emotions head-on, to sit with them, and to let them flow through us. Similarly, laughter amid pain is not a sign of denial, but a testament to the human spirit's ability to find moments of joy even in the darkest times.

The Dance of Grief and Growth

Resilience is about finding your path through grief, recognizing your unique strengths, and drawing on support in ways that resonate with you. What works for one may not work for another. Grief and growth are two faces of the same coin. It's hard to imagine experiencing pain without eventually finding a path to personal growth. As you navigate the stormy seas of sorrow, remember the strength you've shown before. Every challenge you've faced, and every tear shed, has added to the reservoir of resilience within you. Embrace this dance between grief and growth, for it is the foundation of your next chapter.

The Beauty of Transformation

Life's most complex challenges, especially the losses we endure, have an uncanny ability to mold and shape our essence. Think about the journey of a diamond. It begins as a simple piece of carbon buried deep within the earth. Over time, under immense pressure and heat, this carbon undergoes a transformation, emerging as one of the most sought-after gems in the world. This process is neither easy nor quick, but the result is a brilliant, resilient stone.

In much the same way, our adversities can serve as catalysts for our transformation. They can refine our core beliefs, values, and priorities. What may initially seem like a setback or tragedy can ultimately strengthen our character. These experiences give us a depth of wisdom, an inner compass that can guide us through future challenges.

The Unfolding Story

In the aftermath of a significant life event, it's not uncommon to feel lost, like a ship without a compass. The familiar landmarks that once guided us may no longer be visible. But within each of us is the innate power to chart a fresh course, to decide the direction our story will take. In these moments of introspection, ask yourself: "What legacy do I want to leave behind? How do I see my best self emerging from this?" It's crucial to remember that every new day presents an opportunity, a blank canvas. You're gifted a fresh page in your life's book with every sunrise. And you hold the pen. The narrative is yours to shape. Will it be one of growth, resilience, and transformation? The choice is yours.

The Bridge of Resilience

While it's essential to honor the past and the lessons it gave, avoid getting trapped by it. The present moment bridges what was and what is yet to come. Anchor yourself in the 'now,' cherishing the blessings it holds. As you do, let your newfound wisdom guide your steps into the future. Resilience isn't just about overcoming; it's about growing and evolving. It's about recognizing the power within you to shape your destiny. As you embark on your next chapter, remember the strength you've harnessed, the lessons learned, and the endless possibilities that lie ahead. Your story is still unfolding, and the best chapters may still be unwritten.

Setbacks: A Rest Stop, Not a Roadblock

There's an unconscious belief that setbacks, especially after intense grief or trauma, are akin to landing on that feared "Go Back to Start" square in Monopoly. However, life's reality is much different and more forgiving. Setbacks are not complete regressions, but mere detours or pauses necessary to our journey's rhythm. Imagine climbing a mountain. If you slip a few steps after a long ascent, you're not sent back to the base; you merely lose a bit of ground, keeping most of your progress. The lessons, memories, and skills gained on the journey remain intact. Every setback reflects how far you've ventured, not an erasure of your achievements.

After a section on the intricate dance between grief and growth, it's essential to recognize that setbacks aren't a rare occurrence but a fundamental part of the dance itself. Occasionally, one step back follows two steps forward. However, this rhythm ensures we're moving, growing, and integrating our experiences. During days when grief feels heavier, or challenges seem impossible, it's tempting to interpret these feelings as evidence of failure. It's easy to be harsh on ourselves, thinking we should've been stronger or wiser. Yet, our resilience — nurtured through past adversities — becomes our beacon in these moments.

Lean into your moments of doubt, not as a self-indictment, but as an opportunity. Embrace them as life, reminding you of the strength and wisdom you've already cultivated. They are lessons in patience, resilience, and hope. They emphasize the importance of compassionate self-reflection, letting you see how far you've come and highlighting areas for further growth.

Indeed, setbacks can feel disheartening, but they're not roadblocks but rest stops. A moment to rest, reflect, recalibrate, and remember the journey's purpose. As with every sunrise after a stormy night, your progress remains, shadows and all. The setbacks are but a brief darkness before the dawn. And while it's fundamental to lean on supportive people, remember to become your best ally. Be kind to yourself, knowing every setback creates an even more significant comeback. As you navigate the fluctuations of grief, setbacks will become less about loss and more about learning. Embrace them, knowing they're part of your journey toward healing, growth, and newfound resilience.

New Beginnings Await

Moving through the process of grieving is a journey that takes you from the depths of sadness to the heights of growth. Although the pain of losing someone will always be a part of who you are, it does not define your entire existence. Instead, it becomes a chapter in the story of your life shaping the details that are yet to unfold. There may be moments of doubt and hesitation along the way. With every small step you take, you show inner strength, resilience, and capacity for renewal. It shows your capacity to heal, envision possibilities, and overcome challenges.

Chapter 9

Pursuit
Finding Clarity Amid Uncertainty

P ursuing clarity amidst uncertainty is an aspect of our changing lives. As we have navigated each phase of the Grief to Growth Pathway, we have examined the ebbs and flows of each part of the journey. We now find ourselves in the sixth phase, "Pursuit," which invites us to break free from self-imposed limitations and explore the vast possibilities beyond our comfort zones.

The Pursuit phase prompts us to break free from our self-imposed limitations and embrace the world's potential outside. This could be the excitement of uncovering a newfound passion, the warmth of an unexpected relationship, or the deep satisfaction of prioritizing personal wellness. But whatever form it takes, it is a testament to our resilience and an affirmation of our purpose.

However, life rarely follows a straightforward course. As we stand at the edge of uncertainty, a mix of anticipation and trepidation fills us when we gaze into the future. Although we might sense where our dreams lie, unpredictable twists fill the path to reach them. Yet, doesn't the beauty of uncertainty propel us forward? It prompts us to pause, reflect on our accomplishments, and gather the courage to continue.

Imagine a scene with the team sport of rowing. Amidst the synchronized strokes and the gentle movement of water, a figure stands as a beacon of guidance - the coxswain. Their position is unique; while every oars person gazes back, the coxswain has their eyes firmly on the horizon. This singular focus, bolstered by their experience, ensures the boat's path remains unwavering, even amidst turbulent waters. In life, too, we must learn to be our own coxswains, to remember our past not as anchors but as lessons. We should use these lessons as a guidepost, leading us through the fog of doubt toward the brighter horizons of growth.

To navigate the vast oceans of life, one must recognize the winds of the past, for they reveal the routes to our desired futures. Embrace the Pursuit. Let it be the phase where you steer your life with wisdom, facing forward but never forgetting the lessons of the past.

The Power of Values, Strengths, and Goals

As we navigate the winding road of life, we encounter moments of triumph and moments of despair. Experiences like losing a loved one, setbacks in our career, or unfulfilled expectations can be significant sources of grief, anxiety, and depression. I've seen how crucial it is to build a solid emotional foundation with personal values, recognized strengths, and realistic goals. This foundation enhances our resilience and equips us to manage setbacks, endure the journey, and continue.

Personal Values: Your Compass in the Storm

Personal values are like a compass; they guide our decisions and serve as a reference point when we get lost. Staying connected to these values, especially during grief and setbacks, is critical. When you know what truly matters to you, it can become easier to navigate through life's challenges. You have a moral compass that helps you stay true to your path, even when the going gets tough. For instance, if empathy and compassion are among your core values, you are more likely to be forgiving and understanding toward yourself when facing setbacks, which aids in quicker recovery.

Personal values are the timeless truths you hold dear, representing your beliefs, ethics, needs, aspirations, and priorities. Values like family bonds, growth, authenticity, and community steer you towards people and pursuits that resonate at your core. Internalizing these convictions creates an inner lifeline back to yourself during disorientation. When stability crumbles in the wake of trauma, values are constant—unaffected by whatever chaos tosses you. By repeating, "This matters most," you can untangle the web of emotions that grief brings. You can move forward intentionally rather than simply reacting by considering which choices align with your values.

If being courageous is one of your core values, a pivotal loss may encourage the brave step of entering therapy or sharing your vulnerability with trusted confidants. If personal growth matters most, your loss could inspire you to seek new environments and experiences to nourish and stretch your development. Values are the roots from which new growth blooms. It's easy to lose touch with your essence in extreme sorrow. Returning to your values, even through simple acts like baking for family or expressing gratitude in prayer, realigns you with your inner compass. When one area of life darkens, your values shine light on what still holds meaning. By repeatedly reflecting on your personal beliefs, they become embedded touchstones. Amidst chaos and transformation, they provide a firm footing in standing tall and face the challenges ahead. When external anchors give way, values remain — reminding you who you are, what fulfills you, and where you want this next chapter to take you.

Strengths: Your Inner Resilience

Understanding your strengths can be a significant source of empowerment. Your strengths are like your hidden superpowers, helping you to face and overcome adversity. You may have excellent problem-solving skills, or your strength lies in connecting with people. Recognizing and using these strengths enables you to navigate life's challenges more efficiently. For instance, a person with problem-solving abilities might analyze setbacks to understand what went wrong and how to prevent similar situations in the future. Someone with strong interpersonal skills might lean on their support network during difficult times, finding comfort and guidance in their relationships. Staying connected with your strengths gives you confidence in your ability to cope and adapt, reinforcing your resilience.

Realistic Goals: Your Roadmap for the Future

Goal-setting is an essential part of personal growth and development. However, it's necessary to set realistic and attainable goals. Realistic goals help you stay motivated and offer a sense of purpose and direction. However, when setting goals, it's crucial to maintain a balance. Aiming too high can cause disappointment and demotivation, while setting the bar too low can lead to complacency. Remember, the aim is to set goals that stretch you yet are within reach.

Endurance for the Journey

The most critical thing when lost in the wilderness is to keep moving. As long as we maintain momentum in a consistent direction, we increase our chances of finding a way out. The same is true when navigating uncertainty after a significant loss. Though the path is unclear, persistence is critical. Cultivating patience and endurance for the journey ahead enables us to find meaning amid the unknown. All journeys have a beginning phase full of excitement, optimism, and eagerness to set out. But enthusiasm can quickly fade when the reality of the distance and difficulty sets in. Distractions and competing priorities arise. Self-doubt creeps in, tempting us to abandon the effort. Maintaining resilience and determination during this challenging period is critical.

Breaking the journey into smaller milestones helps boost morale when the final destination seems impossible. Scheduling regular check-ins and tracking progress through journaling fosters a sense of momentum. Sharing goals and difficulties with trusted companions provides accountability and encouragement to persevere.

The Reluctant Runner

You could count the marathons I've run on one hand precisely because I've only run two. You might assume from this tally that I'm a seasoned runner, but that couldn't be further from the truth. Instead, I consider myself a defiant jogger—someone who isn't particularly fast but is obstinate enough to keep pushing until that looming finish line is behind me. The story of my first marathon isn't your usual tale of disciplined training, a precisely calculated diet, and months of mental preparation. It's a little more... impulsive. Picture this: a Sunday morning crowd, a naysayer, and a challenge that I couldn't run even four miles. Sounds like the start of a joke, right? But to me, it was anything but.

While many take up marathon running to achieve personal best, overcome their limits, or fulfill a bucket-list dream, my entry into the marathon world was more unorthodox. Driven by an overwhelming desire to prove a point (and perhaps a bit of ego), I signed up for a half marathon. I mean, how hard could it be? I believed in my heart that stubbornness and determination could easily trump a couple of months of training. The day before the race, I stumbled upon a book filled with tales of brave souls who took the leap of running a marathon for the first time. Their stories of courage, humor, and sheer insanity stirred something within me. Why settle for half when you can have the whole? And thus, 13.1 miles became a daring 26.2.

Joining me on this mad adventure was Rod, my marathon-trained friend. I thought, "Stick with him as long as possible and just see what happens." But, as they say, best-laid plans often need to be revised. The marathon route, an old refurbished railroad track, stretched endlessly ahead, 13.1 miles in one direction and

13.1 miles back. No crowd, no cheering, no relief from the overwhelming weight of solitude and self-doubt.

As the miles wore on and I crossed the halfway mark, every step resonated with my folly. A stretch of uneventful silence surrounded me, making each mile feel twice as long. Mile 17 approached, and so did 'the wall.' For those unfamiliar, it's the marathoner's figurative beast when energy diminishes and every fiber of your being screams for rest.

Hitting the Wall

Hitting the wall refers to the mental state where you reach a point of exhaustion while running, causing your body and mind to compel you to slow down or come to a halt. During this phase, your legs feel burdensome and inflexible, making it challenging to find motivation to continue. Every step demands an immense amount of effort. When I reached this point, I allowed myself to walk for a few minutes to recover. After my self-imposed time limit, I tried to run again. It felt like a disconnect between my brain and my legs. As much as I wanted to run again, my body had other plans. I continued this mental and physical tug of war for the remaining 9 miles.

The connection between hitting the wall in a race and the grief journey might sound unrelated. However, many similarities exist regarding people's mental, emotional, and physical challenges. Let's break down some of these parallels:

Mindset and Attitude: A marathon runner's mindset and attitude provide the determination to push past the wall. Their passion for completing the race, beating a personal record, or simply proving to themselves that they can overcome obstacles propels them forward. Similarly, individuals navigating grief must cultivate a mindset that acknowledges pain while embracing hope and resilience. This positive attitude can help one see through the darkest times and seek light again.

Lessons in Vulnerability: When runners hit the wall, they face their vulnerabilities. It's a humbling experience but also makes the journey more authentic. Grief, too, reveals our vulnerabilities, forcing us to confront emotions and memories head-on. This vulnerability, while painful, can also pave the way for deeper connections with others, fostering empathy and understanding.

Learning and Adapting: Every marathon provides lessons for the next. A runner who hits the wall will reflect on what led to that moment and adjust their training or strategies accordingly. Similarly, as we navigate various life losses, we learn more about ourselves, our strengths, our triggers, and our coping mechanisms. Each experience, while unique, prepares us for future challenges.

Whether it's the physical and mental exhaustion of hitting the wall during a marathon or the emotional and spiritual journey of navigating grief, these experiences teach us about resilience, strength, and the power of the human spirit. With the right tools, support, and mindset, we can not only push past these challenges but also grow from them, discovering deeper dimensions of our capabilities. So, my journey began not as an athlete in the prime of their training but as a challenger fueled by sheer will, proving that sometimes it's not just about the pace but the story that takes you to the finish line.

Consistency in the Journey

In navigating uncertainty after loss, consistency provides comfort. When external reality feels unstable, establishing regular rituals and routines can provide a sense of grounding. Pursuing a steady course ahead, despite the challenges, allows incremental progress. Like tending a garden—with dedication, tiny seeds of intention blossom into healing.

Setting regular times for reflection, journaling, exercise, or other wellness practices creates structure. Even when motivation is low, sticking to the routine helps maintain momentum. Sharing our plans with others provides loving accountability. Check-ins with both personal and professional support along the way reinforce consistency.

To avoid feeling overwhelmed, we break large goals into manageable daily targets. Fulfilling our intentions, however small, breeds confidence to keep going. Tracking progress through journal entries or apps helps quantify our consistency. Celebrating each milestone traveled keeps energy and spirits high. Of course, no journey is without detours and pit stops. Self-compassion is critical when confronted with setbacks or delays. Rather than perceiving them as failures, we recognize they are intrinsic to any growth process. Refocusing with care and patience gets us back on course. A supportive community empathizes with struggles and nudges us forward.

Grief often arises in waves, so staying flexible helps us ride these tides of change. Adjusting expectations and reworking plans is sometimes required. Listening intuitively to our needs at the moment and responding accordingly keeps us aligned with internal truth. Through consistency and commitment, small choices accumulate into transformation. Each devoted step carves channels, gradually revealing the path ahead. Progress flows through these deepening grooves like water, gaining momentum and direction. Moving with purpose and consistency through uncertain terrain, we inevitably find our way downstream.

Embrace the Process

Embracing the Past, Thriving in the Present

Loss leaves us sifting through the ashes of our past, searching for pieces to carry forward. Holding the fragments too close can burn and blind us, obscuring the possibilities ahead. Yet letting go completely severs our roots, leaving us adrift, untethered from meaning. Moving through grief with grace involves integrating the past into the present in a mindful way that fosters growth. Rather than rupturing the connection, we aim to transform it. Doing so means honoring its essence through ritual and remembrance while creating space for new experiences. Setting aside sacred times and places for reflection allows us to soak in nourishing and comforting memories. Outside these moments, diverting our energy towards meaningful goals and relationships cultivates a sense of purpose.

Studies show that acknowledging loss and imagining positive possibilities for the future are essential to healing. Visualizing the unfolding story of our lives with hope and intention helps pull us forward, even amid heartbreak. Envisioning your best self and living out core values creates a compass for growth.

Exercising gratitude for the gifts of the past fosters optimism. Flipping through old photo albums reminds us of how we've grown and changed. The resilience and wisdom we've gained equip us for whatever comes next. Believing in second chances and rebirth empowers us to embrace new horizons.

When memories flood unexpectedly, we invite them in with tenderness rather than push them away. Sitting with the bittersweet feelings honors their validity. We speak gently to ourselves, extending the same compassion as a close friend. Reassurance that better days lie ahead emerges through listening deeply to our needs in that moment.

Thriving does not require removing our past to be pain free. Growth means weaving together memories and possibilities to craft a beautiful mosaic. Each minor act of self-compassion, expression, and discovery leads us one step closer to re-engaging meaningfully with life. Mindfully integrating past and present allows us to anchor ourselves in gratitude while setting sail toward fulfilling new experiences.

Embracing New Beginnings: Turning Loss into Growth

Standing at the edge of the void left in the wake of loss, the path seems shadowed and uncertain. Will the darkness consuming everything familiar ever lift? While turning back is impossible, stepping into the unknown requires courage and faith. Yet, with time and care, you may see loss not as an end but as the start of a bold new adventure.

Begin by envisioning your life story as a never-ending book with many volumes left to write. Loss only concludes a single chapter, not the entire narrative. When we close one cover, another waits to be opened. Seeking hope, meaning, and purpose in the present continues to unfold your story.

Now is the time to reconnect with your core values. What matters most to you will illuminate which fresh paths align. Use this inner wisdom as a compass guiding your choices. Taking steps in alignment with your values creates a path towards a future that reflects your truest self. Moving forward also requires flexibility and openness to learning. Have the willingness to experiment with different routes and adapt your course as circumstances evolve. View missteps not as failures but as progress. Each experience will teach you something valuable. Stay curious about what you may still discover.

Appreciate this transition as an initiation into deeper authenticity. Loss strips away comforting illusions, revealing both the ephemeral and the eternal. With less clinging to past identities and achievements, space opens within to uncover presence. Finally, trust you will build resilience and gain an empowering perspective as you integrate this loss into your story. This journey continues...keep turning the page.

Cultivating Stillness Through Rituals of Remembrance

Recovering from loss requires embracing new experiences, relationships, and pursuits. Yet amidst active grief, stillness is also essential. Rituals of remembrance root us in the present while honoring the past, weaving together memories to provide continuity and context for our unfolding story.

Lighting candles or sitting in silent meditation in spaces associated with your loss can help consecrate memories. By eliminating distractions, you can fully immerse yourself in commemorating and experience a sense of calm and clarity. Journaling, drawing, or creating art captures feelings and pays homage to meaningful moments. Compiling memory books, photo albums, or playlists preserves important artifacts and snapshots that bring comfort.

Sharing your creative expressions and stories with others continues the legacy.

On special occasions, observing cherished traditions can evoke fond memories and create warm moments of reminiscence. Prepare their favorite recipes, watch cherished films, and return to meaningful places. You might leave an empty seat at the table to acknowledge their absence.

Stillness is not avoidance of active grief, but regular integration of precious memories into the present. Designating intentional spaces and intervals of quiet reflection provides foundations of peace from which we can expand into life. Through mindful remembrance, the calm eye of the storm comes into view.

Moving forward after loss winds a course between pain and possibility. We gain strength, perspective, and gratitude by fully engaging each emotional wave. The verdant shores of meaning reveal themselves to those willing to dive deep into life's waters. Renewed purpose calls us forward. Though the way may wind through uncharted territory, we never travel alone.

The journey of finding clarity amid uncertainty after loss winds an unpredictable course between grief and growth. By fully engaging each emotional wave while integrating the past and creating new rituals of remembrance, we gain strength, perspective, and gratitude. Despite the obscurity of the road ahead, embracing patience and resilience during the journey unveils the hidden significance. Seeking external guidance provides accountability, motivation, and course corrections to stay on track. By developing inner resilience, we can learn from setbacks and reconnect with our core values, fostering a sense of hope and possibility. By consistently moving forward with courage and self-compassion, we learn to trust the process.

The impact of loss on our lives is undeniable, yet the degree to which we emerge whole again rests on our readiness to fearlessly explore the depths of existence. Each experience of surrendering to change unfolds latent wisdom and brings us closer to our essential nature. Embracing the teachings of the past and fearlessly embracing the present, we chart fresh paths that resonate with our purpose.

There will be periods of confusion, heartache, and longing when the familiar shores of our past seem to recede from view. With time, acceptance evolves into empowerment and significance. We may even consider loss a catalyst for seeking authenticity, connection, and fulfillment at life's core. Memories, values, and strengths illuminate our path ahead, guiding us through life.

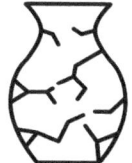

Chapter 10

The Beauty in Brokenness

Experiencing grief and loss crushes us, leaving us feeling like our lives have fractured into a million little pieces. The feeling is much like a piece of pottery knocked off a shelf, now lying in fragments on the floor. But what if we could learn to see the beauty in this shattered state? What if these breaks and fractures, these places of grief and loss, could enhance our life story rather than end it? That's where the beautiful concept of Kintsugi comes in.

Kintsugi is an ancient Japanese art form, its name translating to 'golden joinery.' When they break a piece of pottery, instead of discarding it or hiding the damage, Kintsugi artisans put it back together with a special lacquer mixed with precious metals like gold. The result? They not only repair the piece of pottery but also transform it into something even more beautiful than before - they highlight and honor the unhidden cracks. Just like Kintsugi, our lives break apart and disperse like a thousand shattered pieces when we experience grief and loss. But what if we could learn to mend these broken pieces, not by hiding the cracks but by illuminating them, recognizing them as integral parts of our life's journey? This is where Kintsugi holds a powerful metaphor for the human spirit and our ability to experience healing and growth.

Kintsugi and Grief

When we experience loss, we often feel the damage is irreparable, and that something has forever shattered our lives. A gaping void and a crack in our existence remain, and the sheer thought of trying to piece our lives back together can overwhelm us. But much like Kintsugi, it's important to remember that our story is far from over. Our lives, post-loss, will never be the same, just as a repaired piece of pottery will never be identical to its original state. But this doesn't mean that they can't be beautiful. The gold-filled cracks of a Kintsugi pottery piece make it unique and precious. Similarly, our 'cracks' and 'scars,' borne out of grief and loss, lend a unique, depth to our life stories.

As part of our Grief to Growth programs, we take participants through breaking and repairing a vessel using this Kintsugi method. As I talked with one person repairing his bowl, he said, "This process is a lot like our life. Whether it is an event or a decision, everything can instantly break into pieces, and putting it back together takes time, patience, and help from others."

Finding New Meaning or Purpose in Life After a Loss

Just as the Kintsugi potter gently reassembles the broken pieces with care and respect, we, too, need to navigate our journey through loss with compassion for ourselves, understanding that the pain we feel is part of the healing process. This is a powerful metaphor for finding new meaning or purpose after a loss. As we reassemble the pieces of our lives, these experiences of loss become the golden seems that bind our existence, creating resilience and strength that we might never have imagined possible. And it's in this transformation that hope surfaces. Just as the kintsugi pottery is not merely 'fixed' but transformed, so are our lives through the grieving process. We develop resilience, finding beauty and strength in our repaired cracks. These golden scars testify to our ability to endure, heal, and continue growing.

Much like Kintsugi, we can learn to see our grief and loss not as an end, but as an opportunity for transformation. We need to permit ourselves to grieve, to feel the pain, and then, little by little, begin putting ourselves back together. We should remember to embrace our scars, for they are the golden seams that reveal our story. Through this understanding, we can appreciate the renewed beauty of our lives, rich with the promise of hope and the power of resilience.

Expressions of Creativity from the Pain of Loss

Art has an incredible power to heal. Many cultures and civilizations have used art to express emotions, especially those that are too deep or raw for words. Creating—painting, writing, music, or any other form of artistic expression—allows us to externalize our internal turmoil, providing a tangible form to our grief. Music has long been a source of comfort and expression for Kari and me. For others, it may not be through creating music, but by having a playlist of songs they find helpful in expressing their feelings. The key is to think in terms of expression rather than simply creating something. Expression allows for both creative and non-creative outlets.

The parallels between Kintsugi and art therapy in grief are clear. The Kintsugi artist takes broken fragments and transforms them into a masterpiece. Similarly, the grieving person can channel raw emotions and memories into art, turning pain into poignant works that resonate with others.

Building and Strengthening Relationships

Loss can create a vacuum, a space that feels vast and overwhelming. The empty chair at the dinner table, the unsent text messages, or the quiet moments once filled with laughter and conversation become daily reminders of the void. Yet, new connections can flourish in this void, or existing ones can deepen.

Our vulnerabilities become clear in the aftermath of loss, but so does our capacity for empathy. We recognize pain in others more readily, and we become more attuned to the fragilities of human existence. This enhanced empathy can foster deeper connections with those around us.

Consider support groups, where individuals carrying their stories of pain come together in a mosaic of grief, comfort, understanding, and healing. Their shared experiences, like the intricate web of golden seams on a Kintsugi piece, bind them together through human connection, strength, and resilience.

Embracing the Holes Left by Loss

Experiencing loss and brokenness often leaves us with a sense of emptiness or longing. The holes left remind us of what we lost and make moving forward challenging. However, embracing the remaining holes becomes a powerful tool for healing and growth. This embrace means recognizing the holes as part of the healing process and seeing them as sources of fresh growth and strength. While the allure might pull you to fill these gaps with mindless distractions or to disregard them altogether, acknowledging and recognizing these holes as part of the healing process allows you to find acceptance and peace. Though these gaps might painfully remind you of your loss, they also act as catalysts for personal growth and transformation. Honor your past, dive into new experiences, and accept the inherent brokenness. By doing so, you turn these voids into valuable opportunities for growth. Just as Kintsugi highlights cracks as a part of an object's unique history, your losses can add depth to your life's story.

Honoring and Remembering

One way to embrace the voids that emerge after you face a loss is to discover fresh methods to honor and commemorate what you've lost. By honoring and remembering, you can keep the memories of the departed or lost alive and maintain a bond of connection and peace. Some ideas to commemorate them might be the setting up of a memorial, donating to a charity on their behalf, or taking part in activities they cherished.

Exploring new ways to honor and remember your loss can infuse the gaps with warmth and uplifting memories. This can help you navigate your grief and uncover the significance of your experiences.

Seeking New Experiences or Opportunities

Another way to embrace the holes left after experiencing loss is to seek new experiences or opportunities that may not have been possible. When a person experiences a loss, their life may feel limited or constrained, and it's challenging to see beyond the pain. However, by seeking new experiences or opportunities, individuals can create a sense of purpose and direction.

For example, someone who has lost their job may use the experience as an opportunity to pursue an alternative career path or start a business. Someone who has lost a loved one may use the experience to become an advocate for a cause or join a support group. Seeking new experiences or opportunities can help individuals find fulfillment and growth after experiencing loss.

Relinquishing the Pursuit of Wholeness

In a world where we constantly strive for perfection and completeness, we often forget that our broken edges, imperfect lines, and scars shape our identity. Grief and life challenges often magnify these imperfections, making us yearn for a sense of wholeness we once felt. But in the journey from grief to growth, there is a moment where we realize that perhaps seeking to be whole again might be an endless quest. In this realization, we find the strength to relinquish this pursuit and understand that our imperfections have immense value.

Understanding the Role of Brokenness

Every individual will face moments of brokenness in their life. It could be because of losing a loved one, a dream that didn't materialize, or a love that left scars. The aftermath of these experiences often leaves us longing—a desire to become whole again, to go back to a time before the pain. However, the journey isn't about turning back time, but about moving forward with an understanding. Brokenness is not a deviation from our story; it's a chapter on its own. When seen in this way, the emphasis changes from striving for wholeness to fostering integration. This perspective shift, although challenging, allows us to embrace our brokenness and see it as a vital piece of our identity.

The Power of Acceptance

Accepting brokenness as part of our narrative involves facing some challenging emotions. It might bring up memories of past traumas, moments of weakness, and times when we felt utterly lost. Yet we find peace and self-acceptance in this confrontation with our past.

By acknowledging and accepting these experiences, we aren't diminishing the pain they caused. Instead, we validate our feelings and experiences, understanding that they have shaped our worldview, beliefs, and identity. With acceptance, we recognize that while we might have emerged changed, our value remains unshaken. We see our resilience, strength, and the depth of our character.

"Fully embracing your life's journey involves accepting the flaws and imperfections, turning them into stepping stones leading us from the pain of grief to the promise of growth."

The Myth of Perfection

The societal standards of perfection often skew our understanding of self-worth. We're led to believe that our value lies in our flawlessness, in our capability to present a pristine image to the world. Yet, beneath this façade lies a truth that we often overlook: being human inherently means being imperfect.

Cultivating Self-Compassion

Imagine tying your worth solely to perfection. It's an exhausting, unattainable goal. Yet, many of us unknowingly walk this path, constantly chasing an ideal. However, true growth and transformation stem not from perfection but from recognizing our imperfections and evolving through them. It's in these flaws and blemishes that our unique narratives take shape. Embrace your imperfections. They form the unique qualities of your life. Instead of shying away or condemning these aspects, welcome them. Why? Because they present an opportunity to practice self-compassion.

Actively practicing self-compassion means acknowledging your flaws, not as failures, but as parts of your journey. It's about seeing yourself through a lens of kindness, much like how you'd view a close friend. Can you imagine criticizing a friend for a mistake? Then why do it to yourself? When we grant ourselves the grace of understanding, we set the foundation for healing. In the warm hold of self-compassion, we mend, grow, and flourish.

Confronting and dismantling internalized beliefs about self-worth is a challenging task. But, as we embrace our imperfections and flaws, a transformation occurs. The chains of self-judgment that once held us captive break, allowing us to experience a peace we might never have known. The pathway from grief to growth is not about erasing our past or pain. It's about embracing every facet of our being and understanding that our brokenness, flaws, and imperfections are integral to our identity. As we relinquish the pursuit of wholeness, we find something far more valuable—a deep sense of self-worth, acceptance, and the courage to move forward, scars and all.

The Courage of Vulnerability

Brené Brown says, "When we own our story and love ourselves during that journey, we undertake the bravest act possible." Sharing our genuine, imperfect selves with others' demands immense bravery and encourages them to reveal their true selves. Embracing our imperfections teaches us we don't suffer or fail alone.

By opening up about our vulnerabilities, we pave the way for others to unveil theirs. Our fragmented experiences might interlock in unexpected ways, fostering deep connections. Instead of separating us, our flaws serve as the golden threads, weaving us together in mutual understanding and shared humanity.

Redefining Success and Growth

Societal pressures often equate success with perfection - the perfect life, perfect self, perfect choices. But rejecting this unrealistic standard can be incredibly liberating. Growth does not mean fixing all our flaws. Instead, it is the gradual process of learning over a lifetime.

With patience and non-judgment, each experience can enhance our wisdom, resilience, compassion, and self-knowledge. We become more comfortable with uncertainty and change. By redefining growth on our terms, we can find success and fulfillment without measuring ourselves against perfection. Our imperfections become trials that help shape us into who we are.

Embracing the Beauty in Brokenness

It is often said that art reflects life, and the ancient Japanese art of Kintsugi resonates deeply with the human experience, particularly when confronted with loss, grief, and trauma. As we journey through the last section of this chapter, let us delve into the transformational power of Kintsugi principles and how they can serve as a beacon of hope during our darkest hours.

Celebrating Imperfections: The Essence of Kintsugi

Kintsugi is not merely a process, but a philosophy. It doesn't just mend the broken but celebrates the repair. To fully appreciate the beauty of this art, one must change the perspective on imperfection and brokenness. Instead of viewing them as flaws, they testify to resilience, survival, and metamorphosis.

Stories Carved in Gold

We each carry tales of heartbreak, pain, loss, and grief. However, like the Kintsugi artisan who does not hide the cracks but fills them with gold, we too can highlight our stories not as tales of despair but as narratives of strength. Each golden seam on a Kintsugi vessel represents a story. And so, every scar and wound we bear is a testament to our resilience, a story waiting to be told, and a lesson for the world.

The Break That Lets the Light In

Trauma shatters, but it also offers an opportunity to rebuild. Much like Kintsugi, the healing process is a meticulous endeavor that demands patience, compassion, and self-awareness. While daunting, this journey leads us to a renewed self-awareness of its strength and ability to overcome adversity. Just as sunlight filters through the cracks of a repaired Kintsugi bowl, the lessons and strengths gleaned from traumatic experiences illuminate our lives. The emphasis isn't on the breakage but on the brilliant transformation that follows. By cherishing our scars and acknowledging the narratives behind them, we redesign pain into purpose.

The Rhythm of Pain and Understanding

Death, loss, and the grief they usher in can feel insurmountable. Yet, when viewed through the lens of Kintsugi, even these intense emotions bear seeds of growth, hope, and resurgence. The essence of Kintsugi teaches us it's not the brokenness that defines us, but how we choose to heal. Grieving is an intimate dance between pain and understanding. As we wind through memories and navigate our emotions, we weave gold through the cracks left by loss, highlighting our innate ability to adapt, grow, and cherish life with a depth we had not previously known.

A Pathway Illuminated in Gold

Kintsugi is more than an art—it's a way of life. We heal and evolve by embracing our imperfections and finding beauty in our brokenness. Our life's journey, punctuated by moments of grief, trauma, and loss, is like a pottery piece touched by the hands of a master Kintsugi artisan. Each scar, each golden seam, tells a story of resilience, love, and indomitable spirit.

Life will break us just as it mends us. But with the Kintsugi philosophy, we learn that we're not broken—we're simply evolving, transforming, and embracing our most authentic selves. Let us step forth, wear our golden seams with pride, and walk the Grief to Growth Pathway with grace and courage, knowing that our scars illuminate our path.

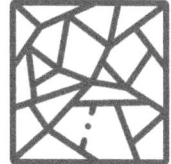

Chapter 11

Life is A Mosaic

L ife is a journey filled with many experiences—some heartwarming, others heartbreaking. We encounter twists and turns, changes and loss. Yet, within this complex and ever-changing mosaic lies the potential for growth and meaning if we approach it with compassion, courage, and wisdom.

We completed our Kintsugi projects during one of our Grief to Growth sessions and took some time to discuss the significance of this process. One participant's stirring testimony beautifully illustrates this profound shift. Her vessel, once whole, had shattered into multiple pieces. As she tried to piece it back together, the challenge was not just the mismatched edges or the extra fragments; it reflected her journey through grief.

"I felt defeated," she confessed. The act of mending her vessel, just like her life after loss, didn't align with her expectations. But a revelation dawned upon her as she wrestled with the misshaped pieces. Though irrevocably changed, her life had gathered layers she hadn't expected. The void left by her loss had inadvertently made space for new relationships and experiences. "These are pieces of my life that I might never have discovered if not for my loss." Not that she was grateful for the heartbreak, but she had found a newfound gratitude for the unexpected patterns of life that followed. Though different, the mosaic of her existence had gained dimensions she hadn't imagined before.

We will explore the inevitability of change and loss in life and the power of the Grief to Growth Pathway in transforming these experiences into opportunities for resilience and personal growth.

The Ever-Changing Nature of Life

Like the changing seasons or the tide's ebb and flow, change is a natural part of life. It can thrill, scare, or jar us. Everyone, including you, endures, evolves, and experiences these shifts. Yet, consider the possibility of seeing your life, even with its challenges, as an astonishing mosaic embellished with dynamic colors and intricate arrangements. This view helps us understand that change and loss are fundamental aspects of life's intricate design.

From subtle shifts in routine to major life transitions, change can take different forms. It can include a career, home, relationships, interests, health status, and more throughout your life. While you embrace some changes, others might be uninvited, leaving you feeling unprepared and caught off guard. Regardless of the life transitions experienced, it is imperative to understand that they are a necessary and inherent part of life, requiring us to learn how to respond in a healthy and productive manner.

One of the most significant changes most people encounter is a change in relationships. Losing a loved one to death, divorce, separation, or estrangement can be incredibly difficult. You may feel intense grief, loneliness, anger, and disbelief. However, it is vital to recognize that these changes can also provide opportunities for growth and new beginnings. For example, after losing a loved one, some people may find solace in volunteering, joining a support group, or pursuing a new hobby. Similarly, people may find new relationships, focus on personal growth, and develop self-reliance after a divorce or separation.

Career changes are another common source of change in life. Losing a job or starting a new one can be exciting and daunting. Losing a job can be deeply painful, leading to anxiety, depression, anger, and a shaken sense of identity. However, it can also provide an opportunity for self-reflection, learning new skills, and pursuing new careers. Starting a new job can be equally challenging, requiring the ability to adapt to a new environment and responsibilities. However, it can also be an exciting time for growth, exploration, and new opportunities.

Changes in health status, either physical or mental health, can also significantly impact one's life. The onset or worsening of the illness can bring frustration, fear, and added stress. The recovery process can build resilience, empathy, patience, and a new appreciation for one's capabilities.

For young adults, going away to college represents a major life transition involving significant changes in relationships, environment, responsibilities, and independence level. While exciting, this time of change can also be anxiety-provoking. However, meeting the challenge head-on, using campus resources, and focusing on personal growth can allow students to thrive.

Later in adulthood, retirement from work can be an enormous change while also opening up new possibilities. Retirement may allow more time for hobbies, travel, and family. Still, it can also lead to feelings of boredom, loneliness, or loss of identity if not approached proactively. Preparing mentally and financially, cultivating interests, and staying socially engaged are keys to a fulfilling retirement.

As discussed throughout this book, it is essential to recognize that the process of change and adaptation is not linear, and individuals may experience setbacks or challenges along the way. However, by developing resilience, engaging in healthy coping strategies, and focusing on personal growth, individuals can find new meaning and purpose in their lives even amidst unwanted change.

Practical strategies for navigating change include being emotionally flexible, practicing mindfulness and stress management, focusing on health-promoting behaviors, actively problem-solving, seeking social support, and maintaining a long-term perspective. Change often allows us to discover inner strengths and abilities we did not know we possessed. With an open, positive attitude, and the right tools, change can become an opportunity for a renewed sense of purpose and vitality.

The Opportunity for New Growth

Change and loss are inevitable, but they offer unique opportunities to grow and develop. One of the most significant growth opportunities adversity presents is building resilience. This means we learn new ways to cope, solve problems, flex our thinking, regulate our emotions, use resources wisely, and remain determined in the face of challenges. By strengthening these traits, we prepare to tackle present and future difficulties.

Facing significant life challenges gives us insight and wisdom. Reflecting on the lessons from these unwanted changes and losses, we understand more about ourselves, others, and our environment. Such reflections can teach us to value the fleeting nature of life, feel more compassion, rethink our priorities, and acknowledge our inner strength. Armed with this wisdom, we can live with more purpose and intent.

Adversity also allows us to form and strengthen relationships. Difficult times can make us appreciate our loved ones more and deepen our social ties. As we go through change and loss, giving and receiving support in relationships enhances their richness. Connecting with people facing similar challenges can bring a sense of unity and lessen feelings of loneliness.

After undergoing significant life changes, many people discover new passions or revisit old ones. This may result in having more time to dedicate to hobbies, creative activities, travel, community service, or personal growth endeavors. Experimenting with new activities and gaining unique experiences can help them keep learning, growing, and finding joy and purpose. Every person reacts to and copes with change differently, but the chance for enlightenment and rejuvenation is always there. We can discover brightness even in the gloomiest times through newfound wisdom, deepened relationships, or ignited passions. By bravely confronting life's challenges, we can surpass our expectations for growth.

Embracing Your Journey

Embracing your life's journey means loving and accepting all of it — the good, the bad, the mundane, and the extraordinary. It means recognizing every experience plays a part in shaping who you are and the life mosaic you create. By embracing your journey, you discover meaning and gratitude in life's twists and turns.

Practicing gratitude every day is an excellent way to embrace your journey. Even amid pain, there are always things to be grateful for, and focusing on these blessings cultivates joy. Gratitude fosters contentment for all you have already instead of preoccupation with perceived lacks. It illuminates life's gifts that may otherwise go overlooked.

Finding meaning and purpose in all your experiences allows you to embrace your journey thoroughly. Reflecting on how each life phase and event shaped you, taught you, and contributed to your growth will enable you to find significance in your most challenging times. Embracing the totality of your journey — all its peaks and valleys — is part of crafting a meaningful mosaic.

It's essential to embrace difficult moments as opportunities to learn and grow stronger. Hardships can develop resilience, wisdom, strength, and compassion once you endure them. By embracing adversity as a teacher on your journey, you cultivate hope, meaning, and the determination to overcome. You gain courage and perspective to emerge wiser and continue forward.

Living in the present helps you embrace your journey as it unfolds. You witness your life's beauty right now when you stay grounded in the current moment—not obsessively reminiscing or worrying about the future. Today's gifts fill you with a deep sense of gratitude. You see new tiles ready to be placed in your mosaic.

Staying present generates peace and allows you to experience each moment of your priceless journey.

Another way to embrace your journey is to focus on living authentically — your most authentic self. You can wholeheartedly embrace your distinctive journey when you stay loyal to your core values and truths, act with integrity, and express yourself genuinely. Living authentically allows you to be fully engaged in your one precious life without regrets.

Embrace your life's journey by cultivating gratitude for every experience. You appreciate how every experience shapes your character and contributes to your soulful mosaic. Your open heart and mind allow you to discover beauty and opportunity everywhere. You understand life's changes provide tiles to arrange into one miraculous work of art—the mosaic of your journey.

The Unfolding Beauty

Life's beauty lies not in avoiding cracks and broken pieces but in appreciating how our strongest, most luminous mosaics integrate them flawlessly. Our richest life collages contain an interwoven thread of dark and light, grief, and gratitude, cracks, and gold. By realizing life's wholeness transcends any single piece, we discover hope.

Each small tile—experiences, relationships, lessons—in our elaborate mosaic is beautifully imperfect. Our flaws and fissures do not prevent our wholeness, but prove the stunning sum we create. So when life shatters another tile, let us gather every sacred shard and fuse it into our ever-evolving masterpiece.

With an expansive perspective, we cherish how life's changes and losses paradoxically fill voids with meaning. Wisdom settles into our cracks, illuminating new paths forward. As we embed our steeled pieces into the mosaic, tragedy transforms into courage, wounds into empathy, and absence into poignant remembrance.

Let us see life's fragile, temporary tiles as pieces passing through our enduring soul's mosaic. Loss is a painful experience, but from the ashes, we rise stronger and more resilient, our spirits gleaming with newfound strength. Our silent, steadfast mosaic holds stories of despair, delight, heartache, and healing. May we embrace its entirety with wonder, humility, and grace, determined to transform every piece into timeless beauty.

Finding Growth Opportunities in Challenging Times

It can be challenging to find meaning in your most painful life events. Trauma, grief, serious illness, and other adversities may seem senselessly tragic. While you should give yourself time and space to feel anger, sadness, confusion, or fear when faced with severe hardships, you can also seek opportunities for growth in the ashes of adversity. Unearthing wisdom from wounds and finding light amid darkness is an extraordinary human capacity, requiring courage, patience, self-reflection, and support. It helps us integrate life's diverse fragments into a meaningful mosaic.

A Journey, Not a Destination

Grief is not an event with a clear beginning and end, but an ongoing journey full of twists, turns, switchbacks, and occasional steps backward. There is no perfect pathway or predetermined timeline for processing loss. The phases of mourning often do not fall neatly into predictable stages, but rather weave together uniquely for each traveler. And there are moments when, just as you feel the anguish lifting, a memory or milestone sends you tumbling backward through anger, depression, and denial once more.

While the messy map of grief may seem unnavigable at times, guideposts such as compassion, ritual, community, and meaning-making can help orient you on this nonlinear road. Understanding mourning as a lifelong journey rather than a finite destination or checklist of milestones is essential. Each singular loss—a parent, a spouse, a child, a friend—changes us irreversibly, and we continually cycle through elements of grief for the rest of our lives. It is crucial to understand that grief is a process that cannot be easily resolved. Nonetheless, it necessitates a gradual assimilation amidst its setbacks and changes.

It may help to envision mourning as a mosaic you revisit and add to over a lifetime. With each pain, you memorialize love and meaning. You carefully gather up the broken shards and make something sacred—not to replace loss or erase grief, but to honor what remains and what you have discovered within yourself.

On your grief journey, you will experience times when you feel lost, when it seems impossible to reconcile the mangled pieces into anything whole, or when you are thrown backward emotionally. In these moments, guideposts like self-compassion, creativity, laughter, and ritual keep you tethered amid the senselessness.

Talk gently as a friend to yourself in moments of despair or lack of progress. Try creatively assembling your mosaic pieces through journaling, collaging art, or music. Allow the gift of laughter when those you've lost would want you to embrace play and joy at times alongside sadness. Develop personal rituals on birthdays or holidays to weave remembrance while moving forward.

By holding space for the entirety of your grief - the messy process, setbacks, and small milestones forward—you allow your mosaic to take shape. You grant yourself patience and discover meaning in the journey versus seeking a resolution. On this winding, lifelong path stained with sorrow and flecked with growth, you gradually create a nuanced memorial mosaic that integrates loss as a part of life to be honored rather than mended.

Living as a Mosaic

Just like a mosaic, our lives are a collection of diverse experiences that come together to form a complete picture. Living as a mosaic involves embracing this diversity, finding meaning amid blessings and hardships, and recognizing our experiences, forever shaping the mosaic of who we are. To live as a mosaic, we must embrace imperfection and change as inevitable. We can examine each piece of our lives — good or bad, beautiful or broken — appreciate its role in our story and use it to create something even more meaningful. We must believe that the sum of life's eclectic parts will form a stunning mosaic.

Living as a mosaic also involves recognizing how every experience shapes our perspective. How we think, view others, see the world—it's all influenced by our distinct set of experiences that form our mosaic. By remembering this, we can develop understanding, patience, and compassion for how others' mosaics shape their outlooks. We can appreciate how our mosaic helps us find meaning and purpose.

This perspective also helps us find beauty in life's broken pieces and the growth that can spring from adversity. Each painful experience—loss, failure, loneliness—represents a fractured tile that can be transformed into wisdom, strength, empathy, and resilience to add to life's mosaic. Living as a mosaic involves openness—to people, ideas, and opportunities, so we continually add interesting fragments to our life's collage. It means embracing uncertainty, change, and new realities. To live as a mosaic is to live courageously, creatively, and wholeheartedly engaged in all that life offers. It is vulnerability, humanity, and accepting imperfection. It is discovering meaning and beauty wherever we can. It is ever-evolving.

Our experiences, sights, sounds, and relationships are the fragments forming our soulful mosaic. When times are dark, we must trust we can use these pieces to create something stunning, just as art is born from what appears broken. But living as a mosaic is a lifelong process. Our work is never done as we pick up each new tile and carefully add it to our masterpiece.

Your Unique Brilliance

Life will surely bring sorrow and unexpected changes that may shatter parts of our identity or worldview. However, by carefully reflecting on lessons learned, reassessing priorities and possibilities, and leaning on others for perspective and strength, we can use these experiences to add additional dimensions and beauty to our life mosaic. Each sorrow and each victory makes us more nuanced, compassionate, and resilient.

Rather than desperately trying to replace what is irreplaceable, you can honor its memory by using the insights gained from your loss to select new mosaic tiles thoughtfully. Your wounds heal into scars with time, signifying your sorrow and strength today. You see how loss and grief polish your character, maturity, resilience, and capacity to live purposefully. Your mosaic becomes more complex, dimensional, and authentic. You learn to balance grief with gratitude, pain with growth, and severance with continuation. You allow your mosaic to be eternally touched by love and loss.

As intricate and unique as a mosaic, our life path contains inherent ups and downs, joys and griefs, failures and triumphs. Yet, through it all, we have the power to assemble the fragmented pieces into something meaningful and beautiful. By actively and compassionately engaging in the Grief to Growth Pathway, we can find light even in our darkest times. Our mosaic becomes a metaphor for healing and discovering possibility and wisdom in life's inherent imperfection and change. Just like mosaic art, our experiences can come together to create something astonishing if we embrace both brokenness and brilliance.

Chapter 12

Your Path Forward

The Ripple Effect of Grief-Driven Purpose

"You will laugh again... and mean it!" My daughter expressed these words, reflecting on what she would say to her younger self following the loss of her mom eight years ago. Experiencing joy after loss often seems impossible, particularly when its overwhelming weight dictates every facet of our lives. Grief operates much like a ripple effect. Imagine a serene pond, reflecting the peaceful surroundings, until a stone breaks the surface, shattering the stillness and creating ripples that spread across the water. Just like that, one unexpected event can shatter our world.

Having just turned fourteen a few weeks prior, I vividly recall a chilling Tuesday morning, the phone ringing with news from the hospital about a sudden change in my father's condition. Merely a day before, we felt assured that he was doing well and would return home soon. But as we arrived at the hospital, my mother's voice broke the silence with two devastating words: "he's gone!" The gravity of that moment further intensified when Pastor Gilmore, the pastor of our local church, approached me. With tears in his eyes, he offered a piece of wisdom I've held onto ever since: "This isn't fair, but your choices now will define your path ahead. You can harbor bitterness or let this pain mold your future." Shortly after my wife's passing, I shared that same advice with my daughters.

Life's milestones often come stamped with past experiences, shaping our reactions like a well-worn path. Through my mom's resilience in the face of my dad's passing, she emerged as my beacon of strength, demonstrating unparalleled courage while leading our family of six children. Alongside the pain of losing my dad were awkward conversations with friends at school and mentors. Their attempts to comfort were often misguided or absent.

Loss is an inevitable part of our existence. My journey through various losses has sharpened my sensitivity to others facing difficult situations. Now, I firmly believe that experiencing loss has enriched my empathy. It's not about having the perfect advice for others. Sometimes, simply being there, fully present, can be the most transformative gesture of all.

Remembering: Embracing Memories and Rituals

The power of memory is undeniable, holding an unparalleled strength in the healing journey after a loss. To remember is to acknowledge the profound absence and honor the deep connections once shared. Each recollection serves as a sanctuary of comfort, a testament to the moments that shaped us, and an affirmation of the lessons that guide us. Yet, as vital as these memories are, establishing rituals to honor them further elevates their significance. These rituals offer therapeutic comfort through memorial services, marking anniversaries, or indulging in personal practices that echo the past. They are not simply the act of reminiscing, but a celebration of what was treasured and an acknowledgment of the life that continues to unfold.

Reflecting: A Dynamic Internal Dialogue

When we reflect, we actively plunge into our emotions and thoughts, striving to understand and embrace them without casting judgment. This process is more than mere introspection; it's a dynamic internal dialogue. We ask questions, search for deeper meaning, and come to terms with change. Reflecting helps us pinpoint how grief has altered our view of life, our priorities, and our core beliefs. Acknowledging these shifts is crucial. It highlights the growth sprouting from our pain. It propels our journey from mourning what once was to wholeheartedly embracing what lies ahead.

Rejoicing: Celebrating Progress and Life

Every individual's journey from grief to growth brims with obstacles. Yet, every hurdle crossed, no matter how minor, warrants a heartfelt celebration. Imagine laughing genuinely for the first time since you experienced a loss or starting a fresh venture inspired by your ordeal. Each moment isn't just a victory; it's a light of progress. In our Grief to Growth program, we actively recognize these beacons. At the beginning of every week, we share our "weekly wins"—the moments that brightened our days or made us beam with pride over our accomplishments.

Rejoicing transcends just our personal achievements. When we rejoice, we exhibit resilience and our ability to unearth joy in the face of sadness. Still, we also boldly declare that we're determined to craft new cherished memories even as we treasure the old ones. Thus, when we celebrate life, it isn't merely about our personal journey. It's also a heartfelt tribute to the ones we've lost, underlining their ripple effect of influence on our path.

Navigating Grief Together: Our Family's Journey

Navigating the intricate maze of grief and loss is a challenging journey, often filled with unexpected twists and turns. It's like walking through a dense forest, unsure of where the path may lead but confident of the destination: healing and understanding. For Kari and me, this path is not one we walk alone. The echoes of loss are magnified sevenfold as we recognize its impact on each member of our blended family.

Our family mosaic is crafted with love, faith, laughter, and shared experiences, but also with the evidence of loss. With my two daughters and Kari's five sons, each child navigates the turbulent seas of grief, guided by their unique compass. Each has their story of loss, their memories, and their triggers. A simple song, a particular scent, or even a cherished family tradition can send emotion coursing through them. It serves as a reminder that grief is a personal yet collective experience. This is our family pilgrimage.

As we wrote this, it's been eight years since Marybeth and Eddie left voids in our lives. My daughters lost their mother to cancer during their teenage years. For Kari's sons, it was an unexpected sudden loss of their father, with ages ranging from seven to 18 at the time of Eddie's passing. While the contours of grief have shifted and evolved, the core essence remains the same. Throughout this book, Kari and I have shared our hearts and the journey towards healing. However, we felt it would be helpful for our children to share their individual journeys of how the loss of a parent has impacted their lives and the growth that they have experienced. Dive into their stories as they navigate the act of remembering and reflecting on their individual experiences, and find moments of rejoicing amidst the pain. Through their eyes, you'll gain a fresh perspective on grief, resilience, and the power of faith.

Breanna: The Power of Emotion and Memory

Losing a parent not only shapes one's understanding of the fragile nature of life but also propels individuals to seek meaning in the void left after loss. Following a cross-country move, starting her first year of college meant facing many life transitions. Adding to that was seeing her mom only a few months later receive a cancer diagnosis and treatments.

Breanna has seen life woven with love, loss, and resilience threads. She admits that losing a parent has affected her significantly: "I would always ask my mom questions about everything from the normal to the profound. That void is apparent even in my Google searches." Breanna's loss changed her perspective on age and milestones. Rather than view them as the inescapable reminder of time's progression, she has learned to view each year as a precious gift.

As Breanna reflects on the days leading up to her mom's passing, she states, "God showed up for me in such a tangible way, even in the midst of grief. During that time, He proved His name, Emmanuel, God With Us. I felt Him with me when a friend brought me coffee on a bad day, a professor asked me how I was doing mid-semester, and a mother figure held me as I cried in her arms. In my pain and tragedy, it would've been easy to blame God, but He was the very One carrying me daily. He was, and still is, truly with me."

"Throughout my childhood, she would give me and my sister small notes of encouragement," Breanna shares. I held onto those papers without realizing how much they would mean to me. It is a way of ensuring that a piece of her mother's legacy lives on. The sting of loss can make us feel like we will never experience happiness or joy again. But when Breanna expressed what she would tell her younger self following her loss, she stated, "You will laugh again and truly mean it." This is a powerful statement of hope. When in the throes of grief, we may feel that restored joy is an empty wish. It doesn't mean we forget the reality of loss, but we choose to embrace the days and years ahead.

In the same way that Breanna's view of God and his compassion for those hurting, Collin shares his transformative experiences that deepened his faith and empathy for others.

Collin: A Revelation of God's Love

The candid reflections from Collin on grief resonate with raw emotion and deep spiritual insight. The sudden loss of his dad during his first year of college has been a transformative journey, shaping his relationship with God and those around him.

This is his account of how his loss led to a powerful transformation:

"Losing my dad sucked and still sucks. Still, God turned that tragedy into a chance to show me He's not a distant dictator who knows I'm in pain and does nothing; He's an intimate Father who has experienced my pain. He has shared the same feeling of grief from loss and walks with me through it. John 11 was a fundamental change for me. Jesus healing Lazarus was an incredible miracle, but the miracle in my life realized that Jesus knew He'd bring Lazarus back to life. However, Mary and Martha's pain and grief still touched His heart, bringing Him to tears. 'Jesus wept' is an incredible example of God's kindness to 'weep with those who weep.' He could've just moved on and said everything will be fine; I will fix it. But He wept first. He sat with them in their pain. He understood and felt their grief and does the same for me."

"If the God of the universe knows my pain in that way and sits with me in it, how could I not do the same for others? Not because I have any unique wisdom to offer, but because they might know the great mercy, kindness, and compassion of the God that sits with them in their grief. Experiencing grief hasn't led me to become an expert at giving advice to others who are facing loss. It's ignited my passion for the grace Jesus offers to all who are hurting and lost. Grief sucks, but it has completely changed how I see God and others."

Collin's journey from grief to growth is helping others heal and move forward in their faith. He now serves on the pastoral team at the church where his dad also served. As we look at Cyle's loss journey, we see the importance of character, hard work, and cherishing memories.

Cyle: Faith, Hard Work, and Memories

Cyle's experience paints a vivid picture of resilience, introspection, and the search for deeper meaning. Losing a parent shapes his everyday existence with valuable lessons. The inevitability of death and the unpredictability of its timing have led Cyle to a greater understanding of life's purpose. He states, "God has a timeline for each one of us." The unpredictability of death serves as a reminder for Cyle to be prepared spiritually.

A recurring theme in Cyle's memories of his father is the value of hard work. With a touch of humor, he remembers his dad's repeated mantra: "Hard work pays off," as if nudging him to work harder. Today, Cyle embodies this teaching and passes it on to others, including his son.

In honoring his father, Cyle says, "The best way that I can celebrate my dad is by simply talking about him and sharing stories with others who didn't know him. He was a wonderful dad. Like all of us, he wasn't perfect, but he taught me valuable principles worth sharing. Now, I buy a fishing pole every Father's Day in his memory." This simple yet powerful gesture is a testament to the enduring connection between father and son.

Navigating the waters of grief and faith, Cyle confesses, "There were moments of doubt where I questioned God's existence and His plan for me. Trust God, be patient, and keep following His path. "

In sharing Cyle's journey, I am reminded of the complexity of grief, the power of faith, and the importance of cherishing legacies. It has been very impactful for Kari and me to read each of our kids' experiences as they navigated this challenging grief process. Alyssa's journey highlights gratitude and the impact of being a faithful friend during times of loss.

Alyssa: Holding Space and Honoring Memories

Alyssa's grief experience, stemming from her mother's untimely loss, has deeply shaped her outlook on life. At a crucial juncture in life, Alyssa deeply felt the void left by her mother's untimely loss, and we cannot underestimate the influence of a mother. This taught her that life is temporary and led her to adopt a "seize the day" attitude, making every moment count. She states, "My mom was in her 40s when she went through her health challenges and passed away. I don't dwell on that happening to me, but I want to make the most of every opportunity. Whether pursuing life goals or simply loving the people around me well. I want to make it count."

In honoring her mom, Alyssa intentionally got a couple of tattoos that have special significance. She said, "When people ask about them, they are like a conversation starter where I can tell them about my mom and who she was. In sharing our story, I feel a sense of pride for myself and our entire blended family. We have all endured tragedy, and instead of allowing that to destroy us, we have responded with resilience and determination to move forward in an honoring way."

Despite her growth, Alyssa admits to facing the challenge of comforting others in their times of grief. Her loss has sometimes left her feeling somewhat conflicted, navigating the delicate balance between her desire to support others and the triggers of recurring emotions. She says, "I remember what people told me when I lost my mom. Some of the comments were counterproductive. I don't want to do that to others. I prefer to sit with them as a silent support and hold space for them while they grieve."

Alyssa has her personal way of remembering significant birthdays or anniversary dates. Whether savoring treats, cherishing a necklace imprinted with her mother's fingerprint, or revisiting her mom's favorite eatery, each act is a soulful tribute. While simple, these rituals are powerful conduits connecting her to cherished memories, ensuring her mother's essence remains vivid in her life. Losing her mother caused Alyssa to grow up faster than most. However, if she could whisper words of wisdom to her younger self, she'd say: "Still find joy in the innocence of childhood, despite the weight of your loss." And now, when told by others that she reminds them of her mom, Alyssa beams with pride. Her mother's spirit thrives in her, a testament to a legacy of love, resilience, and grace.

As parents of children who have experienced loss, Kari and I feel it is essential to give support and the space for them to process their experience. It is also worth noting that each of our combined seven children navigated their grief in their own unique way and timing. Just because you may not see signs outwardly, they are experiencing the impact of loss. Please don't shy away from hard conversations with your children. Make sure you communicate to them you love and accept them without conditions. In doing so, you can nurture an environment for healing and growth.

Alyssa's narrative underscores a poignant truth: Though difficult, grief can be transformative. Next, we will hear Camden's account of losing his dad and how establishing daily habits can set the course for moving forward.

Camden: God At The Center

In the wake of personal loss, Camden's heart has been deeply molded, giving way to a greater sensitivity and an empathetic outlook toward others. The pain of losing someone close isn't just a concept for him, but a lived experience that has instilled a heartfelt compassion. "When I hear of someone grieving or with a loved one in pain," he says,

"I have a heavy heart for them, and it makes me sensitive to the fact that losing someone is so difficult. I constantly go back to the importance of being anchored in my faith. Without a solid foundation, tragedy and loss can cause us to unravel."

Camden honors his dad in personal ways. Trips to Yosemite, for instance, aren't just mere visits for Camden. Each time he visits is an opportunity to reminisce about the family hikes orchestrated by his dad — memories he once took for granted but now treasures deeply. Daily routines also serve as gentle reminders of his father's presence. Camden has fond memories of his father's morning routine. Camden chuckles, "He would sit in his recliner, sipping the third brew from the same Keurig pod and listening to worship music during quiet reflection. I have implemented this same morning routine of reading my Bible and worship music, but with fresh coffee." It's a testament to the lasting impact of his dad's small, everyday habits — a legacy of peace, reflection, and spiritual connection.

Camden offers simple yet insightful advice to his younger self: "Keep God first in your life." This is a reminder that faith and consistent spiritual disciplines can be the anchor one needs when navigating the complex seas of grief and loss. Through Camden's account, we sense the transformative journey of a soul wrestling with loss but finding strength in faith, legacy, and cherished memories.

Clayton: Reflection and Responsibility

When Clayton reflects on the loss of his father after just turning thirteen, it's apparent how deeply this life-altering event impacted him. "Looking back on losing my father and how it has affected the way I look at life," he states. "I understand it has affected my outlook more than I thought compared to when it first happened." Clayton encountered many crossroads because of his father's absence during crucial, formative years.

Clayton says, "Without my dad by my side, some lessons came the hard way," he states, "and I became very independent. There are some things that I determined I could figure out on my own." Yet, amidst the cocoon of self-dependency, a sensitive heart emerged. Through his loss, Clayton gained insight into others' experiences. He states, "I've gained a better sense of empathy towards others and the things they may go through. Knowing what it feels like to experience a significant loss can put things into perspective and help you put yourself in other people's shoes." The pain he endured became a bridge to understanding the battles others face.

A big change in Clayton's life was his newfound appreciation for the people he cared about. The abrupt loss of his father became a poignant reminder that we have no guarantees, compelling him to cherish every moment with loved ones. However, in retrospect, Clayton admits to the stormy phase that followed his father's death. Clayton offers wisdom and understanding to his younger, more vulnerable self: "You're not the only one experiencing this loss. Remember, those around you are experiencing grief too." He acknowledges times when grief clouded his judgment. "In my grief," he says, "I sometimes used my pain as an excuse, allowing me to justify decisions."

Clayton's reflections depict the personal growth of a young man who faced loss and gained insights into himself, life, and love. His story is a powerful reminder that regardless of age or type of loss experienced, we need to lean on others in our community for support and direction. The last story of our seven children is from Colton. His story is a unique journey of loss, yet it resonates with the hope found in family and friendship.

Colton: Friendship and Family Traditions

In the tapestry of our blended family, where each thread tells a story of resilience and hope, the narrative of our youngest, Colton, stands out with its innocent wisdom. The world, as Colton perceived it, underwent a stark transformation, having lost his dad at the tender age of seven. Significant loss and life transitions had marked Colton's journey up to that point. Kari and Eddie were in the adoption process of Colton at the time of Eddie's passing. While this marked another deep loss in his young heart, Colton found security, love, and acceptance in the family bonds. He holds a special place in our family of seven children.

Colton has a tender and empathetic heart for others' hurting, having known and experienced loss. He has his own unique way of cherishing the memories of his father. Going hunting with his brothers reminds Colton of times with his dad, reinforces the significance of family, and provides a loving and accepting environment. Though brief, his reflection is a powerful reminder of a child's resilience. In Colton's journey, we see the promise that even in the wake of significant loss, with proper guidance, young souls can blossom into beacons of empathy and strength.

The Family Blend

As we give you a look into our family's journey, it is important to recognize that our grieving didn't stop when Kari and I remarried. In fact, those transitions of experiencing new phases of our journey can be a reminder of the loss that we have previously experienced. You can see in each story the uniqueness of their grieving process. Even when grieving the same loss, we express it in unique ways. As parents, we can place expectations on our children to grieve like we grieve.

Embrace the Process

As our relationship was beginning, Kari and I talked a lot about our late spouses and the values that were important to us. A common value that we both held was our faith and the importance of family. With having teenage kids, our priority was to parent them in a way that allowed space to grieve and continued to honor our losses.

My mom remarried a few years after my dad passed away. My step-father was an incredible man and taught me a lot about life that I didn't fully recognize until after Marybeth passed away. It was a difficult transition for me when my mom remarried. As the youngest of six kids, I was the only one still living at home and I struggled with understanding why she needed someone in her life. If you're thinking, "Matt, that is selfish," you would be correct. After leaving for college, I developed a new appreciation for him. I remember being home for holiday gatherings and it was (and still is) a common tradition for everyone to hang out in the kitchen. Following our meal, we tell stories about our days growing up. In between the teasing of each other, we would always throw in some funny stories about our dad. The significant lesson for me was seeing Gabe, our step-dad, laughing right along with us and embracing our family's shared history. I mentioned earlier about my mom being a hero and role model to me. There are many reasons for that, but the conversations that I had with her after my wife passed away are ones I will always cherish. She modeled how to grieve with grace, fully embrace the past, and take steps toward the future.

After Kari and I were married, I was on a business trip to New York and dealing with the impact of grief. That day would have been my late wife's 50th birthday. I felt guilty because I wasn't able to be with my daughters to honor that special day with them. Later that evening, Kari sent me a text message that moved me to tears. It was a video of Kari and the girls were singing Happy Birthday to Marybeth and blowing out candles on a cake. For our blended family, we have embraced the process. As we do this, we are saying to each of our kids, "your story matters and you don't have to hide your grief." I honor Eddie in the same way that Kari honors Marybeth.

This isn't a journey that Kari or I chose. However, we have made the choice that we will move forward with purpose and not waste the pain that we have experienced. This mutual understanding and respect has deepened our bond and helped us navigate the complexities of blending our lives and memories.

Charting a Purposeful Path Ahead

In your journey forward, it's crucial to understand the significance of living with intention, especially after traveling through the six phases of the Grief to Growth Pathway. Living with intention means making conscious choices that propel us toward healing and growth. Just as this book has explored diverse facets of our experience with loss, remember that it's truly about your unique narrative. By living intentionally, you set specific goals and priorities, steering the direction of your life's narrative.

Passivity can often feel like handing over the pen to someone else, allowing them to script your life's story. Your personal story is a testament to this; think of how grief and loss have shaped you. Amidst the hazy aftermath of a loss, living with intention asks, "What now is my purpose, and how do I intend to pursue it?" Our response to this becomes the compass guiding our actions and strategies.

In moving forward, two pillars stand tall:

Our Core: Our core values, faith, and inner beliefs form the very foundation of our intentional journey. We're sometimes challenged to recalibrate and redefine these connections post-loss, but they remain the essence of our directional path.

Our Community: Your community is a source of support, understanding, and growth. It's the people you choose to surround yourself with who uplift, challenge, and guide you. They are the voices that resonate when you're lost and the hands that hold you when you're down.

With all its heaviness, grief can anchor us in sorrow or become the propulsion for our journey forward. Your next chapter might encompass a reshaped routine, a rekindled purpose, or a reconnection with your core values.

As you ponder upon the course of your life's journey, consider these guiding questions:

What values will light your way forward?

Who are the cherished companions of your journey?

How will you ensure a life lived with purpose and direction?

Tell Your Heart to Beat Again: A New Dawn of Hope

There came a moment after the tragic loss of my wife when frustration consumed me. All the hopes, dreams, and future goals I once had seemed completely shattered. One morning, as I was preparing for work, I received a text from a mentor. This mentor, Sherry, had experienced the sudden loss of her husband. Both Mike and Sherry Massey held a significant place in Marybeth's life, as they served as pastors of her local church during her teenage years. Sherry had actually introduced me to Marybeth at a youth camp when I was fourteen. That morning, she shared a song that had impacted her and asked me to listen to it. The song was **Tell Your Heart to Beat Again**. As I listened to it, the words of the second verse caught my immediate attention.

"Beginning - just let those words wash over you.
It's all right now; love's healing hand has pulled you through.
So get back up, take step one, leave the darkness, and feel the sun.
Because your story's far from over, and the journey's just begun."[1] [2]

A whirlwind of emotions engulfed me as I listened — from the sting of tears to a budding hope. In that poignant moment, I felt a reassuring nudge for the first time since my loss. The plans and purpose for my life didn't go away when Marybeth died; instead, I was on the brink of embarking on a new chapter and season. If you're at a crossroads, wondering what's next, I urge you to draw inspiration from this song. Let its words serve as a beacon, reminding you that your story is far from complete. Your journey toward growth and rediscovery has only just begun.

The Grief to Growth Pathway is not an endpoint, but a beacon guiding you toward a purposeful tomorrow. As you move forward, remember that the pen remains in your hand. Your story is uniquely yours, to be penned with conviction, purpose, and intention. Here's to your next chapter; may it be written with hope, resilience, and growth.

---

1. **Tell Your Heart to Beat Again** | Copyright © 2014 Awakening Media Group (ASCAP) (adm. at CapitolCMGPublishing.com) All rights reserved. Used by permission.

2. Listen to the full song, "Tell Your Heart To Beat Again, as recorded by Matt Perkins on the Art of Life CD. https://grieftogrowth.org/book-bonus

Legacy

There are two specific people we would like to acknowledge and honor. Their passion for life, family, and serving people has made a lasting impact that will continue to live on.

MARYBETH PERKINS
1969 – 2015

EDWARD CRAIN JR.
1976 – 2015

STILL LOVED · STILL HONORED · STILL CHERISHED

Matt, Marybeth, Breanna, and Alyssa Perkins

*Eddie, Kari, Collin, Cyle, Camden, Clayton, and
Colton Crain*

Gratitude

We want to express our heartfelt thanks to the countless individuals and organizations that have supported our journey. This journey, marked by the profound loss of our spouses, has been a path of both deep grief and unexpected growth. Our road was not one we walked alone; it was shared with friends and family who stood by us both before and after our losses. Although expressing our gratitude in words is challenging, we want to recognize some individuals who have supported and encouraged us during this transformative season.

Ben Rodriguez, your direction, contribution, and passion for this book project have been encouraging and inspiring. We are thankful for you and your friendship.

To our families, who have stood with us in the darkest times and celebrated the new chapters in our lives. Perkins, Henry, Steiner, and Crain families.

To the staff and congregations who have loved, supported, and stood with us through the most difficult days in our lives. You have shown what a supportive community looks like.

Pastor Dale & Joni Oquist and Peoples Church, Fresno, CA
Pastor Steve & Jean Williams and NorthPointe Church, Fresno, CA
Pastor Carl & Alice Stephens and Faith Assembly, Orlando, FL

Brad and Jana Liebe - Thanks for walking this road with us. You've been there, the good, the bad, and the beautiful. We will always be grateful.

The Grief to Growth Leadership Team - Thank you for your commitment to seeing people take the next step in their journey of loss.

To the many leaders, mentors, and friends:
Jared Anderson
Elvis Aparicio
Sherry Massey Brussaly
Larry & Laura Clark
Anthony Diaz
Mark & Shauna Diaz
Greg & Jill Gill
Mackie Gostanian
Gary Grogan
Mark Gungor

Arni & Jan Jacobson

Brenda Lieder

Christy & Kevin Manning Family

Gordan & Carol Mularski

Patti & Ronnie McDougall Family

Bryce & Denise Paup

Greg & Di Perkins

Frank & Tara Ralls

Christy Rocca Family

Shea & John Sawyer Family

Josh & Stephanie Smith

Kelley & Craig Smith

John Wilds

Rod & Michelle Zimmerman

The Art of Life Cancer Foundation

Byron | Raphael LLP

Faith Worship Arts

McCormick Barstow LLP

Terry Walling | LeaderBreakthru

About the Authors

Matt and Kari Perkins, the heart and soul behind the Grief to Growth® movement, are more than just founders; they are beacons of hope for countless individuals navigating the stormy waters of significant loss. They have become influential voices in grief support due to their personal experiences and commitment to helping others.

Married in 2017, Matt and Kari have blended their lives, passions, and talents, creating a unique synergy that resonates deeply with those they help. In the Central Valley of California, their family life is vibrant and bustling, with seven children as they continue to expand their impact.

Matt Perkins brings over three decades of influential leadership in various church communities across the United States. His remarkable journey as a vocalist and director is marked by producing many impactful musical productions and developing choirs that have graced stages with Grammy-winning artists. In addition to his personal projects, Matt's vocal talents have been featured in productions by Walt Disney Music® and Sony Music®. His commitment to artistic excellence extends beyond performance; as a creative leader and coach, he has developed programs designed to enhance creative leaders' capabilities, helping them realize their full potential.

Kari Perkins shares this musical talent, her voice harmonizing with Matt's, both in life and in their shared recordings. Her presence adds a profound depth to their joint endeavors, both musically and in their mission with Grief to Growth®.

Together, Matt and Kari Perkins embody a rare blend of vulnerability, authenticity, and artistic talent. Their resources, speaking engagements, and extensive musical background have provided comfort and inspired and uplifted individuals from all walks of life. In "The Grief to Growth Pathway," they offer their insights, experiences, and compassionate guidance to all those who find themselves on the difficult journey of grief, providing a pathway to growth, healing, and hope.

Resources

As you reach the conclusion of "The Grief to Growth Pathway: A Guide for Transforming Your Loss into Renewed Purpose," we hope the words on these pages have provided you with guidance and comfort. Your journey, however, does not have to end here. Matt and Kari Perkins and the Grief to Growth® community offer a range of resources to further support and enrich your journey through grief and toward growth.

The Grief to Growth Pathway Workbook: This self-guided companion to the book is designed to deepen your understanding and application of the principles discussed. Through reflective exercises and practical activities, you can personalize your pathway to healing and growth.

Small Group Curriculum and Leader Guide: For those who find strength in shared experiences, our Small Group Curriculum offers a structured way to explore the themes of the book with others. The Leader Guide provides tools and tips for facilitating meaningful and supportive group discussions.

Grief to Growth® Journals: Journaling can be a powerful tool for processing emotions and tracking your journey. Our specially designed journals complement the themes of the book and offer prompts and space to reflect on your personal experiences.

Online Courses: Dive deeper into specific aspects of grief and growth with our range of online courses. These courses offer flexibility and can be a great way to continue your journey at your own pace, with expert guidance from Matt and Kari Perkins.

Music: Discover music resources from Matt and Kari Perkins, offering comfort, hope, and inspiration as you navigate your path of healing and growth.

Engage with Us Further

Grief to Growth® is committed to helping those impacted by the loss of someone or something significant. If you would like to schedule a seminar for your organization or have Matt and Kari Perkins speak at your event, we welcome you to visit our website for more information and to explore the possibility of bringing this transformative message to your community.

Visit us at: https://grieftogrowth.org

Your journey through grief is uniquely yours, but you don't have to walk it alone. Let the resources from Grief to Growth® be your companions as you transform your loss into renewed purpose and strength.

Bonus Content

For related music and creative resources mentioned in this book,
visit https://grieftogrowth.org/book-bonus

▶️
youtube.com/@grieftogrowth

📷
instagram.com/mygrieftogrowth

f
facebook.com/mygrieftogrowth

Thank you for allowing us to be a part of your journey!

Grief to Growth® is a registered trademark. Unauthorized use of this trademark is prohibited.